JE

IN THE

SMALL STUFF

Laughing, Learning, and Living with Jesus Daily

GERALDINE E. WATSON-MARRIOTT

HCP
BOOK PUBLISHING
Professional Publishing. Lasting Impact.

ISBN: 978-976-97708-4-3 (paperback)

Dedication

This book is for anyone who has ever questioned whether the small things really matter.

I've learned that God doesn't only move through big miracles or dramatic moments. He shows up in quiet decisions, ordinary days, and the moments we usually overlook. He's present in whispered prayers, unseen struggles, and the steady faith it takes to keep going when life feels routine.

This book is for those who pray even when no one notices, who believe even when nothing feels extraordinary, and who trust God one day at a time. Every small step of faith, every act of kindness, and every moment of patience matters to Him.

I'm grateful for the simple moments God used to teach me -- the ones that didn't seem important at the time but ended up shaping my heart. Most of all, I give honor to Jesus, who walks with us through the small things and reminds us that nothing in our lives is too small for His love.

Acknowledgments

First, I thank God for placing this book on my heart and giving me the strength to see it through. There were times when the process felt overwhelming, but His presence never left me. He carried me when I felt tired and guided me when I felt unsure.

I am deeply thankful for my loved ones who supported me with prayers, encouragement, and patience. Your love and belief in me have meant more than you know.

To my family: my daughters, Nicole, Jenelle, and Tatyana; my sons-in-law, Joshua and Kamar; and my ten grandchildren, Yvonne, Khloe, Nehemiah, Jeremiah, Michael, Journi, Mia, Ayden, Bryson, and Trinity—thank you for being such a precious part of my life.

To my siblings and other family members who are always only a phone call away with words of encouragement, I am truly grateful. I also want to thank my RFICC family, Restoration of Faith International Community Church, for your continued encouragement and prayers.

To Juliet and Pauline, who have inspired me on this writing journey, thank you from the bottom of my heart.

I'm also grateful for every person who encouraged me, spoke wisdom into my life, or showed kindness along the way. Each interaction, lesson, and season played a role in shaping the message of this book.

To everyone who reads these pages, thank you for allowing my words into your space. My hope is that you feel encouraged, comforted, and reminded that God cares about every detail of your life -- even the ones that seem small.

Preface

So much of life is spent moving quickly from one moment to the next, rarely pausing long enough to notice where Jesus may already be present. We often look for Him in the extraordinary while overlooking the quiet places where He faithfully meets us day after day. Yet it is within the routines, the interruptions, and the seemingly insignificant details that He is gently at work, shaping us with purpose and care. This book is an invitation to slow your pace, to pay attention, and to recognize that God is deeply involved in the everyday moments of your life. It encourages you to rest in the stillness, trust Him in seasons that feel ordinary, and believe that nothing surrendered to Him is ever wasted. As you journey through these pages, may your heart become more aware of His nearness and your faith strengthened by the reminder that Jesus often reveals Himself most clearly in the places we least expect--and in the moments when we need Him most.

Introduction

Life is loud. Our days are filled with endless responsibilities, distractions, and demands that pull our attention in every direction. In the middle of all that noise, it can be hard to sense the nearness of God. Many of us quietly wonder if Jesus is far away - observing from a distance while we struggle through ordinary days that feel anything but spiritual. We search for Him in the dramatic, the miraculous, the mountaintop moments, assuming that if He is at work, it must look big and obvious. But what if we've been looking in the wrong places?

What if Jesus has been closer than we realize--woven into the fabric of our everyday lives? What if He is present in the small moments we rush past, the emotions we try to ignore, and the routines we think don't matter? What if He meets us not only in moments of celebration, but also in disappointment, fatigue, and quiet longing? This book was written as an invitation to slow down and look again. Within these pages, you are invited to notice Jesus in the ordinary spaces of your life--in conversations that seem insignificant, in seasons that feel repetitive, and even in the messes you wish you could erase. You'll discover how He gently fills grace into daily moments, how He redeems what feels broken or wasted, and how He speaks through details we often overlook. This is not a story of perfection or constant spiritual highs, but of a faithful Savior who walks with us through the everyday.

As you journey through this book, my prayer is that you will begin to recognize His presence more clearly. That you will learn to pause long enough to see the evidence of His footsteps in places you once thought were empty. That the familiar parts of your life will begin to feel sacred, and the routines you once dismissed will become holy ground.

May these pages gently remind you that Jesus is always at work; shaping, restoring, and drawing you closer to Him, even when you don't feel it or see immediate results. May you come to trust that nothing in your life is too small for His attention, and no moment is wasted in His hands.

This book is simply an invitation to notice Him, to discover that Jesus has been in the small stuff all along.

Table of Contents

Dedication iii
Acknowledgments iv
Preface vi
Introduction vii
CHAPTER 1: Jesus Lives in the Ordinary 11
CHAPTER 2: Surviving Is Sacred 20
CHAPTER 3: Jesus Speaks Through Quiet Moments 28
CHAPTER 4: Daily Bread, Daily Grace 40
CHAPTER 5: Jesus Sees Invisible Tears 48
CHAPTER 6: Small Strength Counts 55
CHAPTER 7: Rest Is Spiritual Trust 62
CHAPTER 8: Healing Happens Slowly 71
CHAPTER 9: Jesus Restores Identity in Pieces 79
CHAPTER 10: Jesus Uses Kind People 87
CHAPTER 11: Joy Can Return in Tiny Moments 95
CHAPTER 12: Jesus Honors Broken Prayers 104
CHAPTER 13: Letting Go Is Also Healing 114
CHAPTER 14: Jesus Rebuilds Confidence Gradually 122
CHAPTER 15: Jesus Is in Daily Decisions 131
CHAPTER 16: Jesus Works Through Routine 139
CHAPTER 17: Jesus Is Present in Work and Responsibility 147
CHAPTER 18: Jesus Uses Waiting Seasons 156
CHAPTER 19: Jesus Strengthens Through Boundaries 165

CHAPTER 20: Gratitude Reveals God's Activity 174
CHAPTER 21: Jesus Builds Stability Through Consistency..... 183
CHAPTER 22: Small Beginnings Matter to God 192
CHAPTER 23: Jesus Uses Personal Stories 200
CHAPTER 24: Jesus Builds New Dreams Carefully................ 209
CHAPTER 25: Jesus Values Faith Over Perfection.................. 218
CHAPTER 26: Jesus Works Through Compassion 227
CHAPTER 27: Jesus Is Creating Something New Quietly 236
CHAPTER 28: Jesus Has Been Present All Along 245
ABOUT THE AUTHOR 254

CHAPTER 1
Jesus Lives in the Ordinary

SMALL MOMENTS. BIG GOD

"God didn't show up in the wind, the quake, or the fire. He came in the quiet. Jesus still builds our strength the same way--through the gentle moments we slow down enough to hear. The stillness isn't empty; it's where His voice becomes unmistakably clear."
SCRIPTURE: 1 Kings 19:11-12

FOCUS: He comes in the whisper--quiet, steady, right where life actually happens.

We often imagine Jesus showing up in the moments that sparkle. The moments we circle on calendars, dress up for, pray over, and prepare to testify about. But the truth is simpler, softer, and far more intimate than that. Jesus lives in the ordinary. He breathes in the spaces we overlook. He moves in the minutes we rush through. He settles Himself right into the rhythm of our everyday lives.

He is not waiting for a perfect moment to arrive. He is already present in the imperfect ones. Jesus lives in the ordinary--the kind of ordinary that doesn't make it into journals or testimonies. The kind of ordinary that feels too small to matter, too routine to notice, too familiar to celebrate. There are moments in life that pass quietly, so ordinary they barely register in our awareness. No announcements, no visible signs, no sense that anything important is happening. Yet it is often in those very moments that God is closest. While we are folding laundry, driving familiar roads, waiting in line, or sitting alone with our thoughts, He is present--steady, attentive, and near. He does not compete with noise or demand our focus. Instead, He speaks softly, trusting that a heart turned toward Him will recognize His voice.

God's truths are not always delivered in dramatic ways. More often, they come as gentle reminders, subtle nudges, or quiet reassurances that settle deep within us. These whispers shape us slowly, teaching us patience, trust, and awareness. They remind us that faith is not built only in moments of great victory or visible answers, but in the everyday choice to listen, to believe, and to remain open to His presence.

When we learn to pay attention, the small moments begin to change. What once felt insignificant becomes sacred. What once felt routine becomes meaningful. We realize that God has been speaking all along--not because we earned His attention, but because He delights in walking with us through every detail of our lives. And as we listen, we come to understand that no moment is wasted, no day is empty, and no quiet space is ever truly alone when He is there.

Yet that is where He chooses to dwell. He is in the quiet of early morning, when the house is still and the world hasn't asked anything of you yet. He is in the soft shuffle of feet on the kitchen floor, in the steam rising from a cup of coffee, in the breath you take before you open your mouth to speak life into someone who needs it.

He is in the laundry you fold, the emails you answer, the meals you prepare, the errands you run, the responsibilities you carry without applause. He is in the sigh you release when you're tired but still show up. He is in the patience you offer when your emotions want to go another way. He is in the courage it takes to forgive, the humility it takes to apologize, the strength it takes to keep going.

Jesus lives in the ordinary because that is where we live. And He refuses to leave us alone in the places where we spend most of our days. He is in the conversations that seem simple but carry seeds of healing. He is in the moments when you choose kindness over convenience. He is in the decision to pray even when you don't feel spiritual. He is in the tears you cry when no one is watching. He is in the laughter that surprises you on a hard day. He is in the way you gather yourself after disappointment. In the way you breathe through frustration.

In the way you choose hope again, even when hope feels fragile. Jesus lives in the ordinary because He is not a distant Savior. He is

Emmanuel--God with us. Not God above us. Not God beyond us. Not God waiting for us to get it together. God with us. Right here. Right now. In the middle of whatever this day looks like. He is with you in the traffic jam. With you in the grocery store. With you in the waiting room. With you in the classroom. With you in the break room. With you in the kitchen. With you in the quiet ache you don't talk about.

He is with you in the places you think are too small for His attention. But nothing is too small for the One who counts the hairs on your head and bottles every tear you've ever cried. Jesus lives in the ordinary because He knows that's where transformation begins. Not in the spotlight, but in the shadows. Not in the celebration, but in the consistency. Not in the miracle moment, but in the daily choosing. He shapes us in the ordinary. He strengthens us in the ordinary. He speaks to us in the ordinary. He loves us in the ordinary.

And when we finally slow down enough to notice Him there, the ordinary becomes sacred. The routine becomes holy. Everyday becomes evidence of His presence. Jesus lives in the ordinary-- and because He does, your life is filled with more glory than you realize. I have learned that the sacredness of life does not usually appear in the moments we would call important or impressive. More often, it meets me in the ordinary flow of the day--when nothing remarkable seems to be happening at all. It shows up in the routines I once rushed through, the small responsibilities I assumed didn't matter, and the quiet moments I barely noticed. Over time, I began to see that these ordinary spaces were not empty or meaningless; they were filled with God's nearness. Life did not become sacred because something extraordinary occurred, but because God was already present in the simple and familiar.

There is holiness in waking up and choosing to begin again, even when the day feels heavy. There is meaning in preparing a meal, offering patience instead of irritation, listening when it would be easier to turn away, and showing up when no one applauds. These moments may seem small, but they are where love is practiced and faith takes shape. The ordinary is where character is formed, where trust is quietly built, and where grace works slowly and steadily. When I pause long enough to notice, I realize that God is not waiting for me in some distant or dramatic moment--He is already here, in the details of everyday life.

The sacredness of life, then, is woven into the ordinary because that is where we actually live. It is where our choices are made, where our hearts are tested, and where compassion becomes more than an idea. What we call ordinary is often the very place where God is doing His most faithful work--transforming us gently, teaching us to see with gratitude, and reminding us that nothing offered in love is ever insignificant. When I learn to honor these small moments, I begin to understand that the ordinary is not something to escape, but something to cherish, because it is filled with the quiet presence of God.

TESTIMONY

The Prayer Before the Day Began

One morning, I woke up with a heavy sense of uneasiness resting on my heart. Before my feet even touched the floor, my thoughts were already running ahead of me--appointments to keep, responsibilities waiting, problems I hadn't solved yet. The day felt overwhelming before it had even begun, and the weight of everything pressing on my mind made it hard to breathe.
Normally, I would have pushed through that feeling and rushed straight into my routine, telling myself I didn't have time to slow down. But that morning, something inside me told me to pause. Instead of letting my anxiety set the tone for the day, I sat quietly and turned my attention to God.

I didn't have the right words or a long prayer prepared. All I did was ask Him to guide me through the day ahead and to replace my anxious thoughts with His peace. There was no sudden emotional shift, no dramatic moment where everything instantly felt better. I simply sat there for a few moments, trusting that God had heard me.
As the day unfolded, I began to notice a quiet change. The same situations that usually stirred frustration or worry didn't have the same hold on me. Things still went wrong. Unexpected problems still showed up. But instead of reacting with stress, I found myself responding with patience and calm.

I wasn't rushing or panicking the way I normally would. Even when challenges arose, I felt steadier--less shaken, more grounded. It was as if God had gone ahead of me, smoothing the path not by removing every difficulty, but by strengthening my heart to face them.

By the end of the day, it became clear that the peace I experienced hadn't come from a perfect schedule or an easy day. It came from that quiet moment of surrender at the very beginning. That small, simple prayer had influenced every moment that followed.

It reminded me that inviting Jesus into our day doesn't always look dramatic or impressive. Sometimes it's as simple as pausing, acknowledging our need for Him, and trusting Him with what lies ahead. When we choose to start our day with Him--even in the smallest way--He walks with us through every detail, offering peace, strength, and guidance along the way.

POEM

Jesus be in my day like, "Girl, chill."
I'm searching for miracles -- He's fixing my bill.
He pops up in traffic when my patience hits nil.
Turns out He lives in the ordinary… saving me from acting ill.

END-OF-CHAPTER QUESTIONS

1. What everyday moments in your life might you usually overlook but could actually hold spiritual meaning?
2. How can you become more aware of God's presence during normal routines like work, chores, or conversations?
3. In what ways do you sometimes expect faith to appear only in big or dramatic situations?
4. What small daily habit could help you stay more connected to Jesus throughout the day?
5. Think about a recent ordinary moment that brought peace or insight -- how might God have been present there?

CLOSING PRAYER

Lord Jesus, thank You for meeting me in the quiet moments and reminding me that I don't have to face each day on my own. When my thoughts race and my heart feels overwhelmed, help me remember to pause and invite You in. Teach me to trust You with the small beginnings of my day, knowing that You care about every detail that follows. Fill my heart with Your peace, steady my spirit when challenges arise, and guide my steps as I move through each moment. May I grow in faith by choosing You daily, even in the simple, ordinary moments. Amen.

CHAPTER 2

Surviving Is Sacred

SMALL MOMENTS. BIG GOD

"You didn't wake up today on your own strength. Mercy carried you here. God's compassion didn't run out yesterday-- it met you again this morning, steady and faithful, right in the middle of your everyday life. Even the smallest moments are held together by a love that refuses to fail."

SCRIPTURE: Lamentations 3:22-23

FOCUS: He notices the pain no one else catches. Every hidden tear is held by Him.

Let me go ahead and say it plainly:

Some days survival is the only thing standing between you and a full-blown situation. Not a moment. Not a mood. A situation. And yet -- here you are. Still standing. Still breathing. Still trying. Still choosing not to throw your whole life in the trash and start over in another country under a new name. That alone is sacred.

People love to talk about thriving. "Live your best life!" "Walk in your purpose!" "Shine bright like a diamond!" Meanwhile, some of us are just trying to shine bright like a 40-watt bulb that flickers when the AC kicks on. And guess what? God honors that too.

Surviving is sacred because it means you didn't give up when giving up felt easier. You didn't disappear when disappearing felt peaceful. You didn't snap when snapping felt justified. You didn't say what you really wanted to say -- and the Holy Spirit is still applauding you for that. Surviving is sacred because it means you kept going even when your energy was on 2 percent and your charger was nowhere in sight. You kept showing up to life -- maybe not glamorously, maybe not gracefully, but faithfully.

Some days survival looks like prayer and worship. Other days it looks like sitting in your car for ten extra minutes because you need to gather yourself before dealing with people. Some days of survival look like quoting scripture. Other days it looks like quoting silence because you know if you open your mouth, you might have to apologize later.

Surviving is sacred because it means God's grace clocked in early and stayed late. His mercy renewed itself before your alarm went off. His strength carried you when your strength called out sick.

You may not have shouted. You may not have danced. You may not have run around the sanctuary. But you survived -- and heaven threw a celebration with your name on it. Surviving is sacred because it means you're still becoming. Still growing. Still learning. Still fighting for the version of you God sees -- even on the days you don't see it yourself.

Let's be honest: Some days you're surviving with faith. Some days you're surviving with caffeine. Some days you're surviving with a playlist that keeps you from losing your mind. Some days, faith doesn't look like confidence or bold prayers spoken out loud. Some days, it looks like barely holding it together, whispering "Lord, help me," and waiting. On those days, strength doesn't arrive all at once--it comes quietly, in small mercies. Sometimes it comes through a phone buzzing in your hand, a message from a friend who had no idea how much you needed those words. "You've got this."

It doesn't fix everything. It doesn't remove the weight or answer all the questions. But it reminds you that you are not unseen, not alone, and not abandoned in the middle of your struggle. It feels like God saying, "I'm still here," using a familiar voice you trust. And somehow, that simple encouragement becomes enough to take the next breath, say the next prayer, and keep moving forward.

I'm learning that God often shows up in these small, ordinary ways--not always with thunder or miracles, but with timely grace that meets us right where we are. Even on the days when survival feels like the victory, He is faithful to provide what we need, right on time. Some days you're surviving with a prayer that sounds like, "Lord… please." And all of it counts. Surviving is sacred because it means you've lived through things that tried to break you. You've endured storms you didn't post about. You've carried burdens you didn't broadcast. You've handled situations that would've taken somebody else out -- and you did it while still trying to be kind. That alone deserves a medal.

Surviving is sacred because it means God is still writing your story. You're not done. You're not defeated. You're not disqualified. You're in process -- and process is holy. You may not feel strong, but you're still here. You may not feel victorious, but you're still moving. You may not feel like a warrior, but you're still fighting. And heaven sees every step. Surviving is sacred because it means you're choosing life -- even when life is choosing violence.

You're choosing hope -- even when hope feels fragile. You're choosing faith -- even when faith feels like a whisper instead of a shout. And when the dust finally settles, you begin to see things differently. The wounds you once wished away don't disappear, but they no longer define you by pain alone. They become quiet testimonies of what you survived and how far God carried you. Every scar tells a story--not of defeat, but of endurance. They remind you that you were stronger than you realized in the moment, and that grace was working even when you couldn't see it.

What once felt like breaking you was, in God's hands, shaping you. His grace wasn't abstract or distant; it was present and real, meeting you in the hardest places and holding you together when you thought you wouldn't make it through. And now, looking back, you can say with honesty and humility: you are still standing, not because life was easy, but because God was faithful. So if today you're not thriving, glowing, flourishing, or floating -- if today you're just surviving -- congratulations. You're doing something holy. You're proving that God's strength really is made perfect in weakness. You're proving that mercy really is new every morning.

You're proving that grace really does carry what you can't. Surviving is sacred. And so are you.

TESTIMONY

The Unexpected Kindness

One afternoon, I found myself weighed down by discouragement. Several things in my life felt overwhelming all at once, and my heart was tired from carrying more than I felt able to handle. I went about my day trying to push through those feelings, but the heaviness followed me into even the most ordinary moments.

As I stood in line at a store, lost in my thoughts, the person in front of me turned around and began a casual conversation. There was nothing remarkable about the words they spoke, yet the way they spoke them mattered. Their smile was warm, and their tone carried a kindness that felt sincere, not rushed or forced. In that brief exchange, I felt a shift inside me.

The interaction lasted only a moment, but it touched me deeply. That small act of kindness lifted my spirit in a way the other person probably never realized. It reminded me that even when we feel invisible or burdened, God sees us. He knows exactly what we are carrying, and He often meets us through the simplest gestures at the most unexpected times.

Moments like that have shown me how God works through ordinary people and everyday situations. He doesn't always use grand miracles or dramatic events to encourage us. Sometimes, He uses a smile, a kind word, or a brief conversation to remind us that we are not alone. In that quiet moment, I was reminded that Jesus is present in the small details of our lives, working through acts of kindness to bring comfort, hope, and reassurance right when we need it most.

POEM

Surviving is sacred, even when I feel worn,
Some days I celebrate just getting up this morn'.
Didn't quit, didn't crash, didn't lose my mind,
That alone feels like victory signed and sealed divine.
God claps for progress the world can't see,
Because making it through is holy victory.

END-OF-CHAPTER QUESTIONS

1. What challenges in your life have required you to simply focus on getting through one day at a time?
2. How has your understanding of strength changed during difficult seasons?
3. In what ways can survival itself be seen as an act of faith rather than weakness?
4. Who or what has helped you keep going when life felt overwhelming?
5. After reflecting on this chapter, how can you show yourself more compassion during hard moments?

CLOSING PRAYER

Lord Jesus, thank You for meeting us in the ordinary moments of our lives. When our hearts feel heavy and our spirits grow weary, You remind us that we are never alone. Thank You for the small kindnesses You place along our path--simple words, warm smiles, and unexpected moments that lift our souls when we need it most.

Help us to recognize Your presence in these everyday encounters. Open our eyes to see how You are working through people, circumstances, and quiet gestures of love. Teach us to trust that no moment is too small for You to use, and no burden is too insignificant for You to care about.

As we move forward, help us to be vessels of Your kindness to others. May our words be gentle, our hearts attentive, and our actions reflect Your love. Use us, Lord, in the small moments, so that others may feel seen, valued, and encouraged--just as You have done for us.

We place our lives, our worries, and our hopes in Your hands, trusting that You are present in every detail. Thank You for walking with us, even in the small stuff. Amen.

CHAPTER 3
Jesus Speaks Through Quiet Moments

SMALL MOMENTS. BIG GOD

"Life gets loud, but God doesn't compete with the noise. He invites us to slow down, breathe, and recognize that He is God right where we are. In the stillness, Jesus reminds us that peace isn't found in control--it's found in surrender."
SCRIPTURE: Psalm 46:10

FOCUS: He catches the tears no one else notices, and in the stillness, He whispers, "Be still and know."

In a world filled with noise, distractions, and constant activity, it can be easy to miss the gentle ways Jesus communicates with us. We often expect God to speak through dramatic signs or powerful experiences, but many times His voice is found in stillness and silence. Quiet moments give us space to slow down, reflect, and become aware of His guidance.

When life becomes calm -- during prayer, reflection, or even a peaceful pause in the middle of a busy day -- our hearts become more open to understanding. Jesus may speak through a peaceful feeling, a thoughtful realization, or a sense of direction that brings clarity. These moments may seem small, but they often carry deep meaning and comfort.

This message reminds us that we do not always need loud answers to know God is present. By creating space for quiet, we allow faith to grow and wisdom to develop. Jesus often works gently, guiding us step by step, reminding us that His presence is steady and reassuring even when His voice comes as a whisper rather than a shout.

Let me tell you something I've learned about Jesus:

He does not always speak in the loud, dramatic, "stop-the-presses" kind of ways we expect. No thunder. No lightning. No angelic choir doing background vocals. Sometimes He speaks in a whisper so soft you almost miss it because you were too busy talking. And that's the problem -- we talk a lot.

We talk when we're stressed. We talk when we're confused. We talk when we're trying to convince ourselves we're okay. We talk when we should be listening. We talk when we should be sleeping.

Some of us talk in our sleep. Meanwhile, Jesus is over there like, "I'll wait." And He does. Patiently. Lovingly. Quietly.

Jesus speaks through quiet moments because He knows that's the only time some of us stop performing. Stop pretending. Stop rushing. Stop trying to fix everything with our own two hands. Quiet moments are where the truth sneaks in. But let's be honest -- quiet moments don't always feel spiritual. Sometimes they feel like you're just sitting there staring at the wall, wondering why you walked into the room. Sometimes they feel like you're hiding in the bathroom for five minutes of peace. Sometimes they feel like you're in the car, parked in your own driveway, gathering yourself before you go inside.

Some days don't feel heroic at all. They feel fragile and unfinished, held together by little more than whispered prayers and small mercies. Faith, on those days, isn't loud or confident--it's quiet endurance. It's waking up, taking a breath, and trusting God for just enough strength to make it through the next moment.

Sometimes it feels like living in the space between breaths--the sacred pause where life slows down and everything feels suspended. In that stillness, when you're forced to wait and can't rush the healing or the answers, God seems to move faster. Not with noise or spectacle, but with intention. His presence becomes more noticeable there, more intimate. Grace keeps working even when nothing else seems to be moving.

And when the dust finally settles, you begin to see what those moments were shaping in you. The wounds didn't disappear, but they changed meaning. The scars you carry are no longer just reminders of pain--they are quiet testimonies of survival. Evidence that you were stronger than you realized and that God's grace was not theoretical, but real and present, holding you together when you thought you might fall apart.

Looking back, you can see how faithfully He met you in the small stuff--in the pauses, the prayers you could barely form, the strength that arrived just in time. You are still standing, not because the journey was easy, but because God was steady.

And Jesus is right there in all of it. He speaks in the pause between your thoughts. He speaks in the breath you didn't realize you were holding. He speaks in the moment you finally stop trying to control everything and whisper, "Lord… I need You." Quiet moments are holy because they strip away the noise -- and let's be real, we carry a lot of noise.

The noise of worry. The noise of opinions. The noise of schedules. The noise of "What if?" The noise of "Why me?" The noise of "I'm fine" when you are absolutely not fine. Jesus speaks through quiet moments because He knows we can't hear Him over all that. Sometimes His voice sounds like peace settling over you for no reason. Sometimes it sounds like clarity dropping into your spirit when you weren't even praying for it. Sometimes it sounds like conviction -- the gentle kind, not the "get your life together" kind.

Sometimes it sounds like comfort that wraps around you like a blanket fresh out the dryer. And sometimes His voice sounds like silence -- not the empty kind, but the kind that says, "I'm here. You're safe. Breathe." Quiet moments are where Jesus does His best work. He calms storms there. He untangles thoughts there. He heals wounds there. He reminds you of who you are there.

He reminds you who He is there. But here's the funny part:

We act like quiet moments are suspicious. We get nervous when things get too still. We start checking our phones, checking our emails, checking the fridge even though we know nothing new is in there. We treat silence like it's a problem instead of a gift. Meanwhile, Jesus is whispering, "Finally. I've been trying to talk to you all day." Quiet moments are sacred because they make room for God. They make room for truth. They make room for healing. They make room for the version of you that's not exhausted, overwhelmed, or pretending. Jesus speaks through quiet moments because He knows that's when your heart is open, your mind is soft, and your soul is listening.

So, the next time life gets quiet -- don't rush it. Don't fill it. Don't run from it. Lean in. Because the Savior of the world might be whispering something just for you. And trust me -- you don't want to miss it. May the quiet moments--the ones that feel slower than you expected and heavier than you planned--draw you closer to the One who speaks peace into your soul. May you come to see those pauses not as interruptions, but as invitations. Invitations to rest, to listen, and to remember that God is often most present when everything else grows still.

May the quiet moments--the ones that arrive unannounced and refuse to be hurried--draw you closer to the One who speaks peace into your soul. May you begin to see those moments not as empty spaces to be filled, but as holy ground where God is already waiting. When life slows you down and the noise finally fades, may you discover that stillness is not something to fear, but something to enter.

In those quiet places, where distractions fall away and you're left with your own thoughts, your unanswered questions, and your weary heart, may you sense His nearness in ways you never noticed before. May His presence feel gentle, not demanding--steady, not rushed. May He meet you without judgment or expectation, offering rest instead of pressure, peace instead of performance.

When your prayers feel simple or unfinished, may you remember that God listens just as closely to sighs as He does to eloquent words. May you learn that silence does not mean absence, and waiting does not mean abandonment. Even when nothing seems to be happening on the surface, may you trust that He is working beneath it--healing, restoring, strengthening you in ways you cannot yet see.

May the quiet moments soften what life has hardened and calm what the world has made anxious. May God speak peace into the places you've been carrying tension, fear, or doubt. Peace that doesn't depend on answers. Peace that holds steady even when circumstances don't change. Peace that settles deep within your soul and reminds you that you are safe, seen, and loved.

And when it's time to step back into the noise--to return to responsibilities, conversations, and the weight of everyday life--may you carry that peace with you. May it steady your steps and shape your perspective. May it remind you that you are never walking alone, and that the same God who meets you in the stillness goes with you into every moment that follows.

May you come to recognize that God often does His most meaningful work in the quiet--in the pauses, the waiting, the spaces between breaths. And may those moments draw you closer and closer to Him, again and again, until peace no longer feels distant, but familiar.

TESTIMONY

The Delayed Appointment

There was a day when I arrived late for an appointment because traffic was far worse than I had expected. I remember feeling irritated and tense as the minutes ticked by. My mind kept replaying everything that was now off schedule, and I assumed the delay had thrown off my entire plan for the day. All I could see in that moment was inconvenience.

As I waited, someone else nearby struck up a conversation. At first, it felt like a simple exchange meant to pass the time, but as we continued talking, the conversation deepened. They shared that they were walking through a difficult season and feeling weighed down by circumstances beyond their control. What surprised me was how open they were, and how much they seemed to need someone--anyone--to listen.

As we talked, the frustration I had been holding onto slowly faded. Words of encouragement were exchanged, and there was a sense that neither of us had been placed there by accident. In that short window of time, something meaningful unfolded. What started as an unwanted delay became a moment of connection, understanding, and mutual encouragement.

Later, I reflected on how differently the situation could have gone if I had remained consumed by my frustration. I realized that what I initially labeled as a disruption had actually created space for something important. If everything had gone according to my schedule, that conversation never would have happened.

That experience reminded me that not every delay is wasted time. Sometimes what feels like an interruption is actually an invitation--to slow down, to notice others, or to be present in a moment we didn't plan for. What I thought was a problem turned out to be purposeful, and I walked away grateful for a delay I once resented.

POEM

Jesus speaks through quiet moments when the noise takes rest, not when I'm scrolling loud, thinking I know best.
When the house gets still and my thoughts slow down,
That's when His whisper gently turns me around.
No thunder needed, just peace so true,
A soft "be still" … breaking right through.

END-OF-CHAPTER QUESTIONS

1. What quiet moments in your day could become opportunities to listen for God's guidance?
2. How do noise and busyness sometimes prevent you from recognizing spiritual clarity?
3. When have you felt peace or direction after taking time to slow down and reflect?
4. What practical step can you take to create more stillness in your daily routine?
5. How might learning to be still strengthen your trust in God's presence?

CLOSING PRAYER

Jesus, I come to You just as I am--frustrated at times, impatient more often than I want to admit, and quick to assume that delays mean something has gone wrong. I like knowing what's next. I like feeling in control. And when my plans are interrupted, my first response is usually irritation instead of trust.

But You see what I don't. You know what You're doing even when I can't understand it. Help me remember that You are present in every pause, every delay, every moment that feels wasted to me. When I'm tempted to rush ahead or complain about what didn't go according to plan, gently remind me to slow down and look around. Teach me to notice the people You place in my path. Give me a heart that is open instead of closed off by frustration. Help me listen more, love more freely, and be willing to step into moments I didn't schedule. Let me see interruptions not as obstacles, but as opportunities You've lovingly arranged.

I give You my expectations, my timelines, and my need to control outcomes. I confess that I don't always trust Your timing, even though You've never failed me. Help me release what I'm gripping so tightly and rest in the truth that You are always working--quietly, intentionally, and with purpose.

Thank You for meeting me in the ordinary places, in waiting rooms and traffic jams, in conversations I didn't expect and moments I almost missed. Help me walk through my days with greater awareness of Your presence and deeper trust in Your plans. I want to be available to You, even when life doesn't go the way I thought it would.

I place this day, and every interruption that comes with it, into Your hands. Amen.

CHAPTER 4
Daily Bread, Daily Grace

SMALL MOMENTS. BIG GOD

"God isn't asking you to carry tomorrow. He's giving you what you need for right now. "Give us this day our daily bread" is more than a prayer--it's an invitation to trust Him one day at a time. Today's strength, today's peace, today's provision… He supplies it fresh."
SCRIPTURE: Matthew 6:11

FOCUS: God meets today's needs with today's mercy. He gives just enough strength for this moment.

This message reminds us that God provides what we need one day at a time. Just as bread nourishes the body, grace strengthens the heart and spirit for daily living. Life often brings new challenges each day, and instead of giving us everything at once, Jesus offers steady support and renewal as we move forward step by step.

Daily grace means that we do not have to be perfect or have everything figured out. Each morning brings another opportunity to begin again, learn from yesterday, and trust that God's mercy is fresh and available. Even in ordinary routines like working, caring for others, or managing responsibilities, His provision is quietly present.

The lesson encourages gratitude for simple blessings -- food, strength, patience, and peace -- that sustain us through everyday life. When we depend on Jesus daily rather than only during crises, we begin to recognize that His care is constant. Through daily bread and daily grace, we learn to live with trust, humility, and appreciation for the small ways God meets our needs.

Let me be honest: When Jesus said, "Give us this day our daily bread," I don't think He meant the kind of bread we try to stockpile like we're preparing for a spiritual snowstorm.

He meant daily -- as in, "You're going to have to come back tomorrow, sweetheart." And that right there is where the comedy begins. Because we love a yearly blessing. A monthly miracle. A lifetime guarantee. But daily? Every day? Consistently? Faithfully? Like brushing your teeth? Whew. That's a lot.

Daily bread means God gives you just enough strength not to lose your mind today. Not tomorrow. Not next week. Not for the whole month. Just today. And honestly, some days that's all I can handle. Daily bread looks like waking up with barely enough energy to roll out of bed, but somehow you make it. Daily bread looks like patience showing up right before you say something you can't take back. Daily bread looks like peace sliding into your spirit like, "Hey girl, I heard you needed me."

Daily grace is the same way. It's not the fancy, dramatic grace we imagine -- the kind that comes with angel wings and a soundtrack. No, daily grace is the grace that shows up in sweatpants. It's the grace that covers you when you're running late. The grace that keeps you from snapping at people who are trying you. The grace that whispers, "Don't send that text," right before you hit send. The grace that reminds you to breathe before you make a scene.

Daily grace is the reason you didn't fall apart yesterday. Daily grace is the reason you're still standing today. Daily grace is the reason you'll make it tomorrow. And let's be real -- some days require more grace than others. Some days you wake up feeling holy. You're humming worship songs, drinking water, minding your business. Other days you wake up and immediately need the Lord, three angels, and a spiritual security team.

But that's the beauty of daily grace -- it adjusts to the size of the day. If the day is small, grace is gentle. If the day is chaotic, grace comes in like a first responder. If the day is ridiculous, grace rolls up its sleeves and says, "Alright, let's get to work."

Daily bread and daily grace are God's way of saying, "You don't have to be perfect. You don't have to have it all together. You don't have to pretend. Just come back to Me every day, and I'll give you what you need." Not what you want. Not what you think you need. Not what you saw somebody else get.

But what you need -- for your life, your personality, your challenges, your calling. Daily bread for your body. Daily grace for your attitude.

So, if today you're not feeling deep, powerful, or spiritually impressive -- if today you're just trying to make it through without crying, cussing, or quitting -- you're right on schedule. Because God didn't ask you to be extraordinary. He asked you to come back daily. Daily bread. Daily grace. Daily you. Daily Him.

And somehow, that's more than enough. There are days when weariness settles deep, when strength feels thin and your heart wonders how much more it can hold. In those moments, may you remember that you were never meant to carry everything on your own. God sees the places where you feel depleted, the quiet exhaustion no one else notices, and He meets you there with steady care.

May you find comfort in the way He provides day by day--not all at once, not far ahead, but faithfully in the present moment. He gives what is needed for this step, this hour, this breath. When you feel weak, may you discover that His strength does not depend on yours. It meets you exactly where you are, filling the gaps you cannot fill yourself.

May your heart learn to rest in that truth. You do not have to be strong enough for tomorrow. You only need to trust that today is held. Even when your energy is low and your prayers feel simple,

God remains sufficient. His presence is steady. His grace is dependable. And His care does not run out.

As you move through the day, may your soul settle into the quiet assurance that you are supported, sustained, and deeply loved. May you find peace in knowing that what you have is enough for now--because He is enough for today.

TESTIMONY

The Gentle Voice

There was a time when I found myself in the middle of a disagreement, and I could feel my emotions rising quickly. I was frustrated, hurt, and ready to respond in a way that would have only added more tension to the situation. The words forming in my mind were sharp, and I knew if I spoke right away, they would come out harsh and unkind.

In that very moment, I sensed an inner nudge telling me to stop. It wasn't loud or dramatic--just a quiet prompting to pause. Instead of reacting immediately, I chose to remain silent. I took a deep breath and gave myself a moment to settle my thoughts and emotions.

That pause made all the difference. When I finally spoke, my voice was calmer, and my words were more measured. The conversation shifted. What could have easily turned into an argument ended peacefully instead. There was understanding rather than conflict, and relief instead of regret.

That simple experience stayed with me. It reminded me that the Spirit often works in the smallest moments of our lives--guiding our responses, softening our tone, and helping us choose peace over pride. Even in ordinary conversations, when we are willing to listen and pause, God is present, quietly shaping our words and our hearts.

POEM

Daily bread, daily grace, that's how I survive,
God feeding my spirit just to keep me alive.
Some days it's faith, some days it's snacks,
Because prayer feels stronger after something to relax.
He blesses my table, mistakes, and pace,
Serving fresh mercy with everyday grace.

END-OF-CHAPTER QUESTIONS

1. What daily blessings do you sometimes overlook that provide strength or comfort?
2. How has God provided for you in small but meaningful ways recently?
3. In what areas of your life do you struggle to trust God one day at a time?
4. How can practicing gratitude change the way you view your everyday needs and challenges?
5. What is one daily habit you can develop to remind yourself of God's ongoing grace?

CLOSING PRAYER

Lord, thank You for being near to me in moments that feel ordinary but carry more weight than I realize. Thank You for caring not only about the big decisions of my life, but also about my tone, my words, and the posture of my heart in everyday conversations. I am grateful that even when my emotions rise quickly, Your Spirit is present, quietly inviting me to slow down and listen.

Teach me to recognize Your gentle promptings, especially when I feel frustrated or misunderstood. Help me to pause before I speak, to breathe before I react, and to invite You into my responses. Shape my heart so that patience replaces impulsiveness, and humility replaces the need to be right. Guard my words, Lord, so that they reflect Your grace rather than my emotions.

Remind me that choosing peace is often a quiet decision made in a single moment. Help me to trust that You are at work even when I remain silent, even when I step back instead of pushing forward. May my responses honor You and bring calm rather than conflict, understanding rather than division.

Continue to make me sensitive to Your Spirit in the small moments of each day. Let my life be shaped not just by what I say, but by how I say it. And may I never underestimate how powerfully You work through simple obedience, quiet restraint, and a willing heart. I place my words, my reactions, and my relationships in Your hands. Amen.

CHAPTER 5
Jesus Sees Invisible Tears

SMALL MOMENTS. BIG GOD

"Not one tear has slipped past Him. The ones you cried quietly, the ones you hid, the ones you didn't have words for-- He has gathered every single one. Jesus holds your pain with a care deeper than you can measure, turning even your hidden sorrow into something He will redeem."
SCRIPTURE: Psalm 56:8

FOCUS: He holds every tear the world never noticed. Nothing you feel is forgotten by Him.

Not all pain is visible to others. Many people carry struggles behind smiles, continuing their responsibilities while quietly dealing with hurt, disappointment, or worry. This message reminds us that even when our feelings are hidden from the world, Jesus fully understands what we are going through. He sees the tears we do not show and hears the prayers we may not even have words to express.

There are moments when people feel alone because their struggles are misunderstood or unnoticed. Yet Jesus meets us in those private spaces, offering comfort and reassurance. His compassion reaches beyond appearances, recognizing the emotional and spiritual burdens we carry each day.

This reflection encourages honesty with God, reminding us that we do not have to pretend to be strong all the time. When we bring our quiet pain to Him, healing begins slowly and gently. Knowing that Jesus sees our invisible tears helps us feel valued, supported, and reminded that no part of our experience is too small or too hidden for His care.

And the truth is… some of my hardest battles never make a sound. Nobody sees the way I hold myself together, or how many times I almost fall apart before breakfast.

Nobody knows the tears that never reach my cheeks, the ones I swallow because life won't pause long enough for me to fall apart properly.

But Jesus does. He sees the tears I hide behind strength. He hears the cries I bury under responsibility.

He notices the moments when I smile so others won't worry, even though my heart is quietly unraveling at the edges.

He reads every ache I refuse to name, every disappointment I try to outrun, every fear I pretend I don't feel.

And He doesn't shame me for any of it -- He just gathers it all like it's precious.

Because to Him, it is. To Him, I am. And somehow, knowing He sees what no one else sees… gives me the courage to breathe again, stand again, and believe again. My invisible tears are not invisible to Him -- and that alone is enough to carry me into tomorrow.

He is not only the God of the moments that demand attention--the breakthroughs, the celebrations, the prayers spoken out loud. He is also the God of the quiet places. The whispers no one hears. The pauses where words fail. The tears that fall when you're alone and don't even have the strength to explain why you're crying. He is present in the prayers you can't quite form, the messages you type and delete, the cries you swallow because you don't know how to let them out.

He is the God who meets you in the honest confession of I don't know how to do this anymore. The God who doesn't flinch at your exhaustion or turn away from your doubt. He sees you exactly where you are--not after you've cleaned things up, not once you've figured it out, but right in the middle of the mess. He sees you in the thick of it, in the unraveling, and in the quiet aftermath when the noise fades and you're left processing what you've survived.

He sees you in the silence and in the chaos. In the waiting and in the wondering. In the moments when faith feels strong and in the moments when it barely feels present at all. You are never overlooked, never invisible to Him. And in every one of those moments, He is enough.

May the truth that Jesus sees even your invisible tears bring peace to your heart today. May you find comfort in knowing that His presence is near, steady and unshaken. And may you rest in the assurance that you are not alone--never forgotten, never unseen, always held.

TESTIMONY

The Song That Changed My Mood

One day, while driving, my thoughts were tangled up in an issue that had been weighing on me for several days. No matter where I went or what I tried to focus on, the same concerns kept resurfacing. I replayed the situation over and over in my mind, questioning my decisions and worrying about how things might turn out. The more I thought about it, the heavier my spirit became.

As I continued down the road, the radio played softly in the background. I wasn't really listening at first, but then a song came on that caught my attention. The lyrics spoke about trusting God in the middle of uncertainty and leaning on Him when life feels overwhelming. It felt as though the words were speaking directly into the thoughts I had been carrying.

With each line of the song, my heart began to settle. The anxious thoughts that had been spinning in my mind slowly quieted, replaced by a sense of reassurance and peace. By the time the song ended, I noticed a change within myself. The worry that had felt so consuming was no longer as heavy, and in its place was a gentle feeling of hope.

That drive reminded me that God often reaches us in ways we don't expect. In the middle of my overthinking and concern, He used something as simple as a song on the radio to remind me that I could trust Him. Even in ordinary moments, God is present--offering comfort, direction, and quiet reassurance when we need it most.

POEM

Jesus sees invisible tears I try to hide,
The ones behind my smile when I say, "I'm fine," with pride.
He notices sighs nobody else can hear,
Even the strong face I wear all year.
He comforts me gently before I fall apart,
Reading the quiet cries inside my heart.

END-OF-CHAPTER QUESTIONS

1. What emotions or struggles do you tend to hide from others but carry privately?
2. How does knowing that Jesus understands your unseen pain change your perspective?
3. When have you felt comfort even though no one else knew what you were going through?
4. How can you become more honest with God about your feelings and struggles?
5. In what ways can you show compassion to others who may also be hurting silently?

CLOSING PRAYER

Lord, thank You for meeting me right where I am, even in the middle of ordinary moments like a quiet drive or a restless mind. You see the worries I carry, the questions I turn over again and again, and the things that feel too heavy for me to sort out on my own. I am grateful that You do not leave me alone with my thoughts, but gently step in to remind me of Your presence.

Help me to recognize Your voice when it comes in unexpected ways. When my mind is filled with concern, teach me to listen for Your reassurance. When fear begins to crowd my heart, remind me that I can place my trust in You. Thank You for the ways You use simple things--like a song, a word, or a quiet moment--to redirect my thoughts and restore my hope.

Lord, help me release what I cannot control and place it fully into Your hands. Replace my worry with confidence in Your faithfulness and my anxiety with peace that only You can give. Teach me to pause, to listen, and to remember that You are always working, even when I cannot see the outcome.

May I grow more aware of how You speak into my daily life and more willing to trust You in every situation. Thank You for walking with me through uncertainty and for reminding me that hope is never far away. I place my concerns, my thoughts, and my future in Your care. Amen.

CHAPTER 6

Small Strength Counts

SMALL MOMENTS. BIG GOD

"God doesn't wait for you to feel strong before He steps in. He meets you right in the weakness, right in the weariness, and pours in power you didn't have on your own. Jesus doesn't just renew strength for the big battles--He restores you in the small, quiet moments when you feel like you're running on empty."
SCRIPTURE: Isaiah 40:29

FOCUS: God empowers the worn-out and lifts the weak. Even the little strength you have matters to Him.

Strength is not always shown through big achievements or dramatic victories. Sometimes real strength is found in small actions -- choosing to keep going when you feel tired, staying kind when you feel frustrated, or holding onto faith during difficult moments. This message reminds us that Jesus values the quiet effort it takes to move forward one step at a time.

Many people overlook their own progress because it does not seem impressive compared to others. However, small acts of courage and perseverance matter deeply. Getting through a hard day, making a wise decision, or choosing peace instead of anger are meaningful signs of growth. These small moments build resilience and shape character over time.

The reflection encourages us to stop minimizing our efforts and recognize that God sees every attempt to do good, even when no one else notices. Small strength, practiced consistently, becomes lasting spiritual strength. Through everyday perseverance, we learn that even the smallest victories are important in God's eyes and contribute to our journey of faith.

And maybe I don't always feel strong. Maybe some days my courage is the size of a mustard seed, and my hope is hanging on by a thread. Maybe I'm showing up with shaky hands, tired eyes, and a heart that's doing its best not to quit.

But God never asked me to be impressive -- He just asked me to be present. He takes the little strength I have left, the scraps I'm embarrassed to offer, and somehow turns it into enough. Enough to stand. Enough to breathe. Enough to take one more step when I thought I had none left in me.

He honors the strength that looks small to others -- the strength nobody claps for, the strength nobody sees. Because He sees it. He counts it. And He calls it holy.

So even on the days when I feel like I'm barely holding on, I remind myself: small strength still counts with God. And in His hands, small strength grows.

Small strength rarely looks impressive. It doesn't announce itself or demand recognition. It often feels fragile, barely noticeable--like something you might dismiss because it doesn't seem like enough. But small strength carries a quiet kind of power. Like a seed pressed into the soil, it may appear insignificant at first, yet hidden within it is the potential for growth far beyond what the eye can see.

God has always worked through what the world overlooks. He pays attention to the offerings others pass by. What feels meager in our hands is never dismissed in His. Scripture reminds us of a widow who brought the smallest possible gift--so small it could have easily been ignored. Yet Jesus saw it. Not because of its size, but because of the faith behind it. Her offering mattered because it represented trust, surrender, and obedience. In God's economy, the measure has never been quantity--it has always been the heart.

Our strength is often the same. Some days, all we can offer is a little resolve. A quiet prayer. The willingness to show up one more time. And even then, it may feel like we're coming to God empty-handed. But God does not require fullness from us. He invites honesty. He welcomes what we have, even when it feels painfully small.
When we bring our limited strength to Him, something sacred happens. He doesn't shame our weakness or ask us to manufacture more. Instead, He meets us there. He takes what we offer--however

small--and breathes life into it. What we place in His hands is never wasted. He multiplies what we surrender. He transforms what feels insufficient into something purposeful.

Our weakness, rather than disqualifying us, becomes the very place where His strength is most clearly revealed. It is often in our tiredness, our limitations, and our inability to hold everything together that God shows Himself faithful. He steps into the gaps we cannot fill and carries the weight we were never meant to bear alone.

"He gives strength to the weary and increases the power of the weak." -- Isaiah 40:29

God does not wait for us to feel strong before He moves. He draws near when we are worn down. He supplies strength not from our reserves, but from His own. And His supply never runs dry.

May you find comfort in knowing that your small strength is not a disappointment to God--it is an offering He gladly receives. May you remember that what feels fragile in your hands becomes powerful in His. And may you rest in the truth that when you bring Him your weakness, He meets you there with strength that is steady, faithful, and more than enough.

TESTIMONY

The Helping Hand

The other day, I noticed someone struggling to carry several bags into their home. You know the kind of moment--you can tell they're trying their best, but it's clearly more than they can handle on their own. I hesitated for just a second, then decided to stop and ask if they wanted some help.

It didn't take long at all. I grabbed a few bags and carried them inside, and within minutes we were done. But what stayed with me wasn't the task itself--it was the reaction. The relief on their face. The sincere gratitude in their voice. It was obvious that what felt small and simple to me meant far more to them than I had expected. As I walked away, I kept thinking about how easy it would have been to keep going, to stay busy, or to assume someone else would help. Instead, that short pause turned into a reminder I really needed. Sometimes the most meaningful moments of faith don't happen in big, dramatic ways. They happen when we notice the people right in front of us and choose kindness in the middle of ordinary life.

That experience reminded me that the love of Jesus is often shown in the smallest ways--in a helping hand, a few extra minutes, or a willingness to be interrupted. We may never fully realize how much those small acts matter, but God uses them to touch hearts, including our own.

POEM

Small strength counts when my energy's low,
Like choosing peace instead of putting on a show.
I didn't run a marathon, just made my bed today,
And heaven still cheered in its own quiet way.
God measures courage in steps, not amounts,
So even tiny victories absolutely count.

END-OF-CHAPTER QUESTIONS

1. What small victories in your life have you overlooked or minimized?
2. How have everyday acts of courage helped you move through difficult situations?
3. In what ways can small efforts lead to long-term personal or spiritual growth?
4. How can you learn to appreciate progress instead of expecting perfection?
5. What is one small step you can take this week that reflects strength and faith?

CLOSING PRAYER

Jesus, thank You for meeting me in the ordinary moments of my day. Thank You for the quiet nudges that remind me to slow down, look around, and notice the needs of others. I'm grateful that You don't ask me to do big or impressive things to reflect Your love--only to be willing, attentive, and kind.

Help me not to rush past opportunities to serve, even when I feel busy, tired, or distracted. Teach me to see people the way You see them and to respond with compassion instead of convenience. Remind me that no act of kindness is ever wasted when it is done with a willing heart and offered to You.

Use my small choices, my simple actions, and my everyday interactions to shine Your light in ways I may never fully see. Shape my heart to look more like Yours, so that through even the smallest moments, Your love can be felt and Your presence made known. I place my day, my words, and my actions in Your hands. Amen.

CHAPTER 7
Rest Is Spiritual Trust

SMALL MOMENTS. BIG GOD

"God doesn't promise an easier path--He promises Himself. "My presence will go with you, and I will give you rest" is His way of saying you're not carrying life alone. Jesus becomes your peace in motion, your calm in the chaos, your rest even while you keep going."

SCRIPTURE: Exodus 33:14

FOCUS: When God says, "My presence will go with you," rest becomes an act of faith. Letting go is how we lean on Him.

Rest is often misunderstood as laziness or inactivity, but spiritually it can be an act of deep trust in God. Many people feel pressured to stay busy, believing everything depends on their constant effort. This message reminds us that choosing to rest is a way of believing that Jesus is still working even when we pause.

When we slow down and allow ourselves to rest, we acknowledge our human limits and recognize that we are not meant to carry every burden alone. Rest gives the mind and heart space to recover, reflect, and reconnect with God's presence. In quiet moments of stillness, peace replaces anxiety, and clarity begins to grow.

This reflection encourages balance -- working faithfully while also allowing time for renewal. Trusting God means releasing control and understanding that progress does not only come through constant motion. By embracing rest as part of faith, we learn that spiritual strength is renewed not only through effort but also through surrender and restoration.

And maybe rest has never come easy for me. Maybe I'm used to carrying more than I should, fixing what isn't mine, and holding everything together like the world might fall apart if I blink too long. But God keeps reminding me that rest isn't laziness -- it's surrender. It's choosing to believe that He's working even when I'm not. It's trusting that the world won't collapse if I put the weight down for a moment. It's letting His presence be enough when my strength is not.

Rest is the quiet confession that I don't have to run everything, solve everything, or understand everything. It's the sacred pause where my soul finally exhales and remembers who's actually in control.

And every time I choose rest -- real rest, the kind that unclenches my jaw and softens my heart -- I'm choosing trust. I'm choosing to believe His promise: "My presence will go with you, and I will give you rest."

So, I end this chapter with this truth settled deep in me: Rest isn't weakness. Rest isn't quitting. Rest is spiritual trust -- and trust is worship. And when I lean into that kind of rest, I find that God has been carrying me the whole time.

Rest is not something we stumble into naturally. It often comes only after we've reached the end of ourselves--after striving has left us tired, after control has slipped through our fingers, after we've realized that holding on tighter isn't helping anymore. True rest begins in the quiet surrender of letting go. It's born in the darkness of trust, where faith doesn't have answers, only open hands.

There is something sacred about the stillness that follows release. When we stop forcing outcomes and quieting our fears with effort, space opens up within us. And in that space, God meets us. Not with urgency or demand, but with presence. His voice, so often drowned out by noise and striving, becomes clearer when everything else grows quiet. It isn't louder--it's steadier. More reassuring. More real.

Stillness invites us to listen in a way we rarely do when life is moving fast. It reveals how much we've been carrying alone and gently reminds us that we were never meant to. In rest, we remember that God is not asking us to figure everything out--He's asking us to trust Him with what we cannot. Rest shifts our focus from our effort to His faithfulness.

Sometimes rest looks like pausing instead of pushing. Sometimes it looks like choosing to sit with unanswered questions instead of rushing toward solutions. It can feel uncomfortable at first, even vulnerable. But it is often in those quiet, unguarded moments that faith grows strongest--not because circumstances have changed, but because our hearts have softened enough to receive what God has been offering all along.

Rest teaches us that we are carried, not because we are capable, but because God is faithful. It reminds us that we don't have to prove our worth through productivity or perseverance. We are held simply because we are loved. And in that truth, trust begins to renew itself--slowly, gently, honestly.

May you find rest in His presence today--the kind that settles your soul and steadies your heart. May it quiet the voices of fear and replace them with peace. And may that rest renew your trust in the One who carries you, even when you are too weary to carry yourself.

TESTIMONY

The Quiet Walk

After a long and draining day, I decided to take a walk. I didn't have a destination in mind--I just needed space to breathe. The evening air was still, and the sky was slowly unfolding into soft shades of color as daylight faded. Everything around me seemed to move at a gentler pace, inviting me to slow down as well.

With each step, my thoughts began to settle. The worries and tasks that had filled my day loosened their grip, and my attention turned inward. I started thinking about the many blessings God has placed in my life--blessings that are easy to miss when I'm rushing from one responsibility to the next. In that quiet moment, gratitude rose in my heart, not because everything was perfect, but because I realized how present God has been all along.

It struck me how often I overlook these simple moments. I spend so much time focused on what still needs to be done that I forget to notice what God is already doing. Yet, in that peaceful walk, I was reminded that God doesn't always speak through loud answers or dramatic changes. Sometimes His presence is revealed through stillness, through reflection, through moments that feel ordinary but are deeply meaningful.

Stepping away from noise and constant activity creates room for awareness. It's in those unhurried moments that our hearts become more receptive. When distractions fade, we begin to recognize God's nearness--not because He suddenly appears, but because we finally pause long enough to notice Him.

That evening reminded me that God meets us in the small spaces of our lives. He walks with us through quiet streets, gentle sunsets, and thoughtful pauses. When we slow down and pay attention, we discover that His presence has been there all along, patiently waiting to be acknowledged.

POEM

Rest is spiritual trust, though I fight taking a break,
I act like the world depends on every move I make.
God says, "Sit down," while I'm planning nonstop,
Learning faith sometimes means simply to stop.
When I finally pause and release the fuss,
I remember He's working… even without me rushing us.

END-OF-CHAPTER QUESTIONS

1. What makes it difficult for you to rest without feeling guilty or worried?
2. How might rest be an expression of trust in God rather than a lack of effort?
3. When have you experienced renewed strength after allowing yourself to pause?
4. What habits or pressures keep you from slowing down and caring for yourself?
5. What is one practical way you can create time for rest and spiritual renewal this week?

CLOSING PRAYER

Heavenly Father,
Thank You for being a God who is near, not distant--a God who walks with us through ordinary days and quiet moments. Thank You for reminding me that I don't have to search for You in grand gestures or dramatic signs, because You are already present in the stillness of my life.

Lord, help me to slow down. Teach my heart to rest in Your presence when the world feels loud and demanding. When my days become crowded with responsibilities, worries, and unanswered questions, gently draw me back to You. Quiet my thoughts so I can hear Your voice more clearly and recognize Your guidance more readily.

Forgive me for the times I rush past Your blessings without noticing them. Forgive me for overlooking the simple gifts You place before me each day--the moments of peace, the gentle reminders of Your love, the small joys that carry deeper meaning than I often realize. Open my eyes to see what You are doing, even when it feels subtle or unseen.

God, help me to trust that You are working in every detail of my life. When progress feels slow, remind me that growth often happens quietly. When answers don't come immediately, strengthen my faith to believe that You are still listening and still moving on my behalf. Teach me patience as You shape my heart through the small, steady moments.

Thank You for walking beside me when no one else sees, for comforting me in ways only You can, and for meeting me in the stillness when I finally pause. Help me to carry this awareness with me beyond this moment--into my conversations, my decisions, and my everyday routines.

May my life reflect gratitude, attentiveness, and trust. Help me to honor You not only in the big milestones, but also in the simple, ordinary moments where Your presence often shines the brightest. I surrender my day, my worries, and my plans into Your hands, trusting that nothing is too small for Your care.

I thank You, Lord, for Your constant love, Your gentle guidance, and Your faithful presence. May I continue to seek You, notice You, and walk with You--one small moment at a time.

In Jesus' name, Amen.

CHAPTER 8
Healing Happens Slowly

SMALL MOMENTS. BIG GOD

"Jesus didn't rush the blind man's healing. He touched him once, then again, letting clarity come little by little. Some breakthroughs arrive slowly, not because God is distant, but because He's working deeply. Even when you can only see "people like trees walking," Jesus is still moving you toward full sight--one faithful step at a time."

SCRIPTURE: Mark 8:22-25

FOCUS: Jesus works in steps sometimes--clarity coming little by little, strength returning piece by piece. Slow healing is still holy.

Healing is often expected to happen quickly, especially after prayer or a moment of realization. However, real healing usually takes time. This message reminds us that Jesus works patiently within our lives, restoring emotional, spiritual, and personal wounds step by step rather than all at once. Growth often happens quietly, through small changes that may not be immediately noticeable.

There are seasons when progress feels slow, and it can be discouraging when pain or struggle does not disappear right away. Yet slow healing allows deeper transformation to take place. Jesus strengthens our hearts gradually, teaching forgiveness, rebuilding confidence, and helping us develop resilience through everyday experiences.

This reflection encourages patience with us and trust in God's timing. Each small improvement, each moment of peace, and each step forward is part of the healing process. When we understand that healing happens slowly, we learn to appreciate progress instead of perfection and recognize that God's work continues even when change feels gradual.

And maybe I wanted healing to be instant -- a moment, a miracle, a clean break from everything that ever hurt me. But God keeps reminding me that some healing comes in layers, not lightning. Some breakthroughs arrive quietly, not dramatically. Some restoration unfolds in steps, not leaps.

And that doesn't make it any less holy. It just makes it real. It makes it sustainable. It makes it mine. Because slow healing is still healing. Slow progress is still progress. Slow steps are still steps -- and God counts every single one. He's not rushing me. He's not disappointed in me. He's not comparing my pace to anyone else's. He's walking with me, patient and present, even when I feel like I'm barely moving at all.

So, I end this chapter with this truth settled deep in my spirit: Healing doesn't have to be fast to be faithful. It doesn't have to be dramatic to be divine. It doesn't have to be complete for God to call it good. Healing happens slowly -- and somehow, that slow work is shaping me into someone stronger, softer, and more whole than I ever imagined. Healing doesn't happen in a straight line, and it rarely comes all at once. It unfolds slowly, often in ways we don't immediately recognize. Some days feel like progress, others feel like standing still, and sometimes it feels like taking steps backward. But healing isn't about reaching a finish point--it's about continuing to walk, even when the journey feels uncertain.

With Jesus, every step matters. Nothing along the way is wasted--not the waiting, not the setbacks, not the moments when you wonder if anything is changing at all. He walks with you through every season of healing, unhurried and patient. He doesn't rush the process or expect you to be further along than you are. He meets you exactly where you are and stays with you there.

Slow healing can be frustrating, but it is also tender. It gives space for restoration to reach deeper places--places that quick fixes could never touch. Jesus works gently, tending to wounds with care, rebuilding trust where it has been shaken, and strengthening your heart little by little. Even when healing feels invisible, His presence is constant.

You are never unseen in this process. He notices every quiet step forward, every tear that falls when no one else is watching, every prayer you whisper when words feel hard to find. You are loved in the middle of becoming, not just when healing feels complete. You are held through every stage of the journey.

May you find peace in allowing healing to take the time it needs. May you trust that even slow progress is still progress. And may you rest in the assurance that wherever you are on this path, you are seen, deeply loved, and securely held by Jesus--today and every day ahead.

TESTIMONY

The Unexpected Phone Call

There are times when discouragement settles quietly into the heart, unnoticed by everyone else. That day, I was carrying heavy thoughts and emotions but chose not to share them with anyone. I went about my routine, outwardly fine, inwardly weary. I didn't pray about it right away or ask for help--I simply sat with the weight, unsure of what to do with it.

Later that same day, my phone rang. A friend was on the other end, calling just to see how I was doing. There was no urgent reason, no special occasion. They simply said they had felt an unexpected pull to reach out, even though they couldn't explain why. In that moment, the timing felt unmistakable. The conversation wasn't long or dramatic, but it was exactly what I needed. Their words brought comfort, lightened my spirit, and reminded me that I wasn't as alone as I had felt.

Looking back, I can see how gently God was working in that moment. He knew what I was carrying before I ever spoke a word. He understood the quiet discouragement I hadn't voiced and met me right where I was--through the kindness and obedience of a friend. Experiences like this remind me that God is attentive to the details of our lives. He often answers needs we haven't spoken out loud, using ordinary moments and willing hearts to show us His care. In the small, unexpected ways, He reassures us that we are seen, known, and never forgotten.

POEM

Healing happens slowly, not overnight fast,
I prayed once and thought all pain would pass.
But God works steady, layer by layer,
Fixing my heart like careful repair.
Some days I'm better, some days I roam,
But every small step is healing coming home.

END-OF-CHAPTER QUESTIONS

1. What areas of your life require patience as healing continues to unfold?
2. How do you usually respond when progress feels slow or incomplete?
3. What small signs of growth or improvement have you noticed recently?
4. How can trusting God's timing help you remain hopeful during the healing process?
5. What is one way you can show yourself kindness while you continue to heal?

CLOSING PRAYER

Gracious and Loving Father,

We come before You with grateful hearts, aware that You are present with us in every moment--both the ones we celebrate and the ones we quietly endure. Thank You for knowing us so completely. You see what we carry in our hearts long before we ever speak it aloud. You understand the discouragement we try to hide, the weariness we push through, and the questions we wrestle with in silence.

Lord, thank You for reminding us that we are never alone. Even when we feel unseen or forgotten, You are near, gently working behind the scenes on our behalf. Thank You for the ways You send encouragement at just the right time--through a phone call, a conversation, a kind word, or a simple act of care. These moments may seem small, but they carry great meaning. They remind us that You are attentive to every detail of our lives.

Help us, Father, to recognize Your hand in these everyday blessings. Open our eyes to see You at work in the ordinary moments, and soften our hearts to receive the love You so freely give. When discouragement threatens to take hold, remind us to turn to You first. Teach us to trust that You are already providing what we need, even when we don't yet see it.

Lord, shape us into people who listen for Your gentle nudges. Give us sensitivity to Your Spirit so that we, too, may reach out to others at the right time. Use us as instruments of Your comfort, encouragement, and peace. Help us to be willing vessels--ready to call, ready to listen, ready to show love without needing to understand the full reason why.

Strengthen our faith when it feels weak. Restore our hope when it feels dim. Remind us that Your timing is always perfect, even when it doesn't align with our expectations. Teach us patience in the waiting and gratitude in the receiving. May we learn to rest in the assurance that You are always working for our good.

Thank You, Lord, for walking with us through every season of life. Thank You for caring about the smallest details and meeting us in ways that feel personal and intentional. As we move forward, help us carry the peace that comes from knowing we are deeply loved, carefully guided, and never forgotten.

We place our trust in You today and always. In Jesus' name, Amen.

CHAPTER 9

Jesus Restores Identity in Pieces

SMALL MOMENTS. BIG GOD

"God doesn't ignore the seasons that drained you. He steps into the places you thought were beyond repair and begins returning what life tried to take. Restoration may not look like the past--it often looks better. Jesus rebuilds in ways that remind you nothing surrendered to Him is ever truly wasted."
SCRIPTURE: Joel 2:25

FOCUS: He gives back what life tried to steal, rebuilding you bit by bit until you recognize yourself again.

Life experiences, disappointments, and mistakes can sometimes cause people to lose sight of who they truly are. Pain, failure, or rejection may leave us feeling broken or unsure of our value. This message reminds us that Jesus does not expect instant restoration. Instead, He gently rebuilds our identity little by little, restoring confidence and purpose over time.

Rather than fixing everything at once, Jesus works through everyday moments -- teaching us new perspectives, helping us release past burdens, and reminding us of our worth. Each lesson, each act of healing, and each moment of growth becomes a piece of the restoration process. What once felt damaged begins to take new shape through grace and understanding.

This reflection encourages patience and self-compassion during seasons of change. God sees the whole picture even when we only see fragments. As Jesus restores identity piece by piece, we begin to recognize that our story is not defined by broken moments but by the healing and renewal that follow. And maybe I didn't notice how much of me had gone missing. How many pieces I handed away to survive. How many parts of myself I buried just to keep moving. Some losses were loud, but most were quiet -- the kind you don't realize happened until you look in the mirror and barely recognize the reflection.

But Jesus does. He sees every fragment I dropped along the way. He knows the parts of me I forgot, the parts I hid, the parts I stopped believing were worth keeping. And He doesn't rush the restoration. He gathers me slowly, gently, intentionally -- like someone handling something priceless. Piece by piece, He reminds me who I am. Piece by piece, He returns what life tried to steal. Piece by piece, He rebuilds the identity I thought was too shattered to recover. And He doesn't shame the brokenness. He doesn't scold the missing pieces. He calls the rebuilding holy. He calls the process beautiful. He calls me worth restoring.

You are not the sum of what slipped through your fingers, the seasons that ended too soon, or the versions of life you had to grieve. Loss may have shaped parts of your journey, but it does not define who you are. God is always doing something deeper than simply replacing what was lost--He is restoring what still matters most. He is writing a story of redemption that continues forward, even when the past feels heavy.

What feels broken to you is not unusable to Him. God does not turn away from the scattered pieces of your life; He gathers them with care. Every fragment carries meaning. Every place that cracked under pressure still has purpose. In His hands, nothing is discarded. What you see as evidence of failure or heartbreak, He sees as material for renewal.

Redemption is rarely loud or instant. It happens slowly, thoughtfully, often in ways we don't recognize right away. God works patiently, reshaping what was damaged and breathing life into what felt beyond repair. He does not erase your story--He transforms it. The broken places remain, but they are no longer signs of defeat. They become proof of His faithfulness and reminders of how deeply you have been held.

God creates beauty in ways we would never choose for ourselves. He brings order where there was chaos, meaning where there was pain, and hope where there was once only loss. The process may take time, and it may not look the way you expected, but His work is intentional and kind. He is not finished with you.

May you begin to see yourself through His eyes--not as someone marked by what was lost, but as someone being shaped by what is being restored. May you trust that every broken piece still has value in His hands. And may you rest in the assurance that God is faithfully at work, turning what once felt shattered into something whole, meaningful, and deeply beautiful.

So, I end this chapter with this truth settled deep in my spirit: I don't have to come to Him whole -- He meets me in the fragments. I don't have to pretend I'm complete -- He's the One who completes me. Jesus restores identity in pieces… and somehow, in His hands, every piece finds its place again.

TESTIMONY

The Lesson in Patience

There was a day when I found myself standing in a long line, growing more impatient with every passing moment. My feet were tired, my thoughts were restless, and I could feel frustration quietly building inside me. I kept glancing ahead, wishing the line would move faster, mentally rehearsing everything else I needed to do once I finally got through.

Then something shifted. Instead of letting irritation control my thoughts, I made a simple choice. I began to pray silently right where I stood. There were no fancy words--just honest conversation with God. I asked Him for patience, for peace, and for the ability to be present instead of annoyed.

As I continued to pray, I noticed my breathing slow and my shoulders relax. The noise around me faded into the background, and the wait no longer felt so heavy. Time didn't suddenly speed up, but my heart softened. By the time I reached the front of the line, the frustration I had felt earlier was completely gone.

That moment stayed with me. It reminded me that patience isn't always about changing our circumstances--it's often about allowing God to change our perspective. What began as an ordinary inconvenience became a quiet moment of connection and calm. In the smallest situations, when we invite Jesus in, even waiting can become an opportunity for peace.

POEM

Jesus restores identity in pieces, not all at once,
I thought I'd wake up holy -- surprise, still a mess for lunch.
He gathers my fragments I tried to hide,
Polishing purpose I pushed aside.
Bit by bit He rebuilds the real me inside,
Turning broken parts into strength and pride.

END-OF-CHAPTER QUESTIONS

1. What life experiences have affected how you see yourself today?
2. In what ways do you feel God may be rebuilding your confidence or sense of purpose?
3. Which parts of your past are hardest to release while healing continues?
4. How can patience help you trust the process of personal and spiritual restoration?
5. What positive qualities or strengths is God helping you rediscover in yourself?

CLOSING PRAYER

Heavenly Father,

Thank You for meeting me not only in the big moments of life, but also in the quiet, ordinary ones. Thank You for reminding me that You are present even when I am standing still, waiting, or feeling unseen. In moments when impatience rises and frustration creeps into my heart, help me to pause and turn my attention back to You. Lord, teach me to see waiting not as wasted time, but as sacred space--an opportunity to breathe, to pray, and to realign my spirit with Yours. When my surroundings feel noisy and rushed, quiet my thoughts and calm my heart. Help me release the need to control every moment and instead trust that You are at work, even when progress feels slow.

Give me patience that goes deeper than circumstance--patience rooted in faith, shaped by grace, and strengthened through surrender. Remind me that peace is not found in getting through life faster, but in walking through it with You. Help me respond to delays with gentleness, to interruptions with humility, and to inconveniences with gratitude.

Jesus, I invite You into the small moments of my day--the lines, the pauses, the waiting rooms of life. Let these moments draw me closer to You rather than pulling me apart inside. Transform my perspective so that what once frustrated me becomes a place where Your presence comforts me.

Thank You for Your constant patience with me. Thank You for Your steady love, Your quiet guidance, and Your faithful reminders that I am never alone. May my heart learn to rest in You, trusting Your timing and embracing Your peace, one small moment at a time.

In Your precious name I pray, Amen.

CHAPTER 10
Jesus Uses Kind People

SMALL MOMENTS. BIG GOD

"A true friend doesn't disappear when life gets heavy. They show up, stand close, and carry what you can't. That kind of steady love is Jesus working through ordinary people--reminding you that you're never walking alone, even in the hardest moments."
SCRIPTURE: Proverbs 17:17

FOCUS: Love shows up through people who stay, support, and lift you. Their kindness is His hands at work.

Kindness is often seen as something small, but it can carry powerful spiritual meaning. This message reminds us that Jesus frequently works through ordinary people who choose to show compassion, patience, and understanding in everyday situations. A simple smile, encouraging word, or helpful action can become a way God brings comfort and hope to someone else.

Many times, we look for miracles in dramatic forms, yet Jesus often meets people through human connection. Kind individuals become instruments of grace, offering support during difficult moments without always realizing the impact they make. Small gestures can lift heavy burdens and remind others that they are not alone.

This reflection encourages us to value kindness as an important expression of faith. When we treat others with care and empathy, we reflect God's love in practical ways. Jesus uses willing hearts, not perfect ones, to spread encouragement and healing, showing that even simple acts of kindness can carry lasting spiritual significance.

And maybe kindness doesn't always look polished. Maybe it doesn't show up with perfect timing or flawless words. Sometimes it arrives in pieces -- a small gesture here, a soft smile there, a quiet check-in from someone who doesn't even know they're being used by God. Because Jesus doesn't wait for people to be whole before He works through them. He uses the ones who are tired, the ones who are healing, the ones who are still figuring themselves out. He uses the ones who feel like they don't have much to offer, the ones who think their kindness is too small to matter.

But He sees every piece of it -- every gentle word, every thoughtful act, every moment someone chooses compassion over convenience. And somehow, those little pieces of kindness become lifelines. They become reminders that God is nearby. They become proof that He still moves through ordinary people doing ordinary things with extraordinary heart. Kindness is quiet in a world that never seems to stop shouting. It doesn't compete for attention or demand to be noticed. It slips in gently, often unnoticed, carrying God's presence into places where noise has worn people down. While the world pushes, pressures, and overwhelms, kindness moves differently--it slows, softens, and listens.

Kindness is how God reminds us that we are still seen when everything around us feels harsh or hurried. It shows up in simple gestures: a patient response, a gentle word, a moment of understanding when judgment would be easier. These small acts may seem insignificant, but they carry a weight far greater than their size. They reflect the heart of a God who meets people with compassion instead of condemnation.

In the middle of chaos, kindness becomes sacred. It creates space for grace to breathe. It offers rest to weary hearts and reminds us that love doesn't have to be loud to be powerful. God often speaks through these quiet moments--not to overpower us, but to reassure us. His voice is steady, calm, and full of mercy, cutting through the noise with truth and tenderness.

When you choose kindness, even when it costs you something, you participate in God's work in the world. You become a vessel for His presence in places that desperately need it. Kindness doesn't fix everything, but it points people back to the One who can. It tells a tired soul, You matter. You are not alone.

May you recognize kindness as one of the ways God is near--both when you receive it and when you offer it. May you hear His whisper through gentle moments in the middle of loud days. And may your heart remain open to the quiet ways He is still speaking, still moving, and still loving in a world that often forgets how.

So, I end this chapter with this truth settled deep in me: Kind people don't have to be perfect to be powerful. They don't have to be whole to be holy. Jesus uses them in pieces -- and those pieces still change lives. Sometimes, those pieces even save them.

TESTIMONY

The Friendly Smile

As I went about my day, I passed someone whose posture and expression suggested they were carrying more than what could be seen on the surface. There was a heaviness about them, the kind that doesn't come from a single bad moment but from something deeper--discouragement, weariness, or perhaps a quiet struggle no one else noticed. I didn't know their story, and I couldn't fix whatever they were facing, but I could acknowledge them. So I offered a simple smile as we crossed paths.

They stopped, looked back at me, and smiled in return. Then they thanked me--something so small, yet spoken with sincerity. That brief exchange lasted only a few seconds, but it lingered with me long after we went our separate ways. It reminded me that people are often longing to be seen, even in the most ordinary moments of life.

That interaction showed me how easily kindness can move from one person to another. A smile may feel insignificant, almost forgettable, yet in the right moment it can interrupt discouragement, soften a heavy heart, or remind someone they are not invisible. What seemed like a small gesture to me may have been a quiet encouragement to them.

Moments like that remind me that God often works through the simplest actions. We don't always need the right words or grand gestures. Sometimes love is expressed through something as gentle as eye contact, acknowledgment, or a kind expression. Those small choices have a way of spreading hope farther than we realize, touching lives in ways we may never fully understand.

POEM

Jesus uses kind people more than we know,
The ones who smile when my patience runs low.
A small "you okay?" can rescue my day,
Like heaven sending help in a simple way.
No spotlight needed, just love that's real,
Because kindness is how His presence feels.

END-OF-CHAPTER QUESTIONS

1. When has someone's kindness made a meaningful difference in your life?
2. How can small acts of compassion reflect God's love in everyday situations?
3. What opportunities do you notice around you to show kindness to others?
4. How can practicing patience and understanding strengthen your relationships?
5. What is one intentional act of kindness you can offer someone this week?

CLOSING PRAYER

Lord Jesus, thank You for reminding me that You are present not only in life's biggest moments, but also in the quiet, ordinary ones I often overlook. Thank You for walking with us through everyday encounters and using simple gestures to reflect Your love. Help me to recognize the opportunities You place in my path--moments where a smile, a kind word, or a small act of compassion can bring light into someone else's day.

Teach me to slow down and pay attention to the people around me. Give me eyes that see beyond appearances and a heart that is sensitive to unspoken struggles. When I feel rushed, distracted, or focused only on my own concerns, gently remind me that love is often expressed in the smallest ways.

Lord, help me to never underestimate the power of kindness. Use my everyday choices--my tone, my words, my actions--to reflect Your grace. Let my life be a quiet testimony of Your presence, even when no one notices and nothing feels extraordinary.

I ask that You encourage the weary, strengthen the discouraged, and comfort those who feel unseen. And when You choose to work through me, give me the humility to serve without expectation and the faith to trust that You are multiplying every small act for Your purpose.

Thank You, Jesus, for caring about every detail of our lives and for meeting us right where we are. Help me to walk closely with You, trusting that nothing done in love is ever wasted. I place this day--and every small moment within it--into Your hands. Amen.

CHAPTER 11

Joy Can Return in Tiny Moments

SMALL MOMENTS. BIG GOD

"Night seasons feel long, but they don't last forever. God weaves His mercy into the dark and His joy into the morning. Even if the turnaround is small, even if it comes quietly, Jesus has a way of bringing light back to places you thought would stay dim."
SCRIPTURE: Psalm 30:5

FOCUS: God doesn't rush joy--He lets it rise slowly, sometimes in the smallest places, but it still comes.

Joy does not always arrive through big celebrations or major life changes. Sometimes it returns quietly through small, unexpected moments -- a laugh shared with someone, a peaceful pause in a busy day, or a simple reminder that life still holds beauty. This message teaches that Jesus restores joy gently, often through experiences we might normally overlook.

During difficult seasons, people may feel like happiness has disappeared completely. Yet God often brings encouragement through small blessings that slowly lift the heart. A kind conversation, a moment of gratitude, or a sense of calm can begin to rebuild hope little by little. These tiny moments become signs that healing and renewal are taking place.

This reflection encourages us to stay open to joy, even when life feels heavy. By noticing and appreciating small blessings, we begin to see how Jesus brings light back into our lives step by step. Joy may start small, but over time it grows stronger, reminding us that hope is never truly lost.

There are days when joy feels so far away that I wonder if it remembers where to find me. The weight of life presses in, and everything bright feels muted, like it belongs to someone else's story. I don't always know how to name that heaviness, only that it settles deep and makes even simple hope feel hard to reach. On those days, I've learned not to force joy or pretend it's closer than it is.

But even then--even when I feel stuck in the gray--God is still working. I don't always see it in big ways. Most of the time, I only notice it later, when I look back and realize He was quietly weaving something beautiful into the mess I thought was beyond repair. He never rushes me. He never demands that I feel better before I'm ready. He meets me where I am and lets joy return gently, in pieces small enough for my tired heart to hold.

Sometimes it comes in ways so ordinary they almost feel undeserving of the word joy. A quiet morning before the day begins. The warmth of coffee in my hands. A song that reaches a place in me I didn't realize was still tender. A message from a friend who has no idea their words arrived at exactly the right moment. None of these moments fix everything--but they remind me that something good still lives here.

At first, those moments feel too small to matter. I'm tempted to dismiss them, to tell myself they don't count because they don't last long. But I'm learning that they are enough. Enough to remind me that my heart can still respond. Enough to let laughter flicker back to life. Enough to stir hope when it feels fragile and worn thin. God knows how carefully joy must be handled after pain, so He brings it back slowly--with kindness.

God has always been a God of the small moments. He doesn't overwhelm me with restoration all at once. He rebuilds joy the way He rebuilds faith--drop by drop, whisper by whisper, heartbeat by heartbeat. What begins as a quiet spark slowly becomes warmth. What begins as a glimmer eventually becomes light. And without realizing it, I start breathing a little easier again.

Joy, I've learned, is not always loud or obvious. Sometimes it's a quiet shift inside me. A subtle loosening of the weight. A moment where the darkness doesn't feel quite as heavy as it did yesterday. It's not a declaration--it's a gentle rebellion against despair. A reminder that God is still writing this story, even when I don't recognize the chapter.

So I'm learning to pay attention. To notice the small joys instead of waiting for the big ones. To receive them without minimizing them. And to trust that these tiny moments are leading me somewhere brighter, even when the path feels slow.

If you're here too, I hope you'll notice them with me. And I hope those small sparks of joy will gently guide you back toward the light--one quiet moment at a time.

TESTIMONY

The Encouraging Hug

One Sabbath, something very small yet deeply meaningful happened--a simple hug from someone at church. It wasn't planned or dramatic, but it reached me in a moment when my heart needed reassurance more than I realized. In that quiet embrace, I felt comforted, acknowledged, and reminded that I was not alone on my journey. There were no words exchanged, no explanations offered, yet God used that brief moment to speak gently to my spirit.

As I reflected on it later, I recognized how often God chooses to show His love through people rather than through signs or miracles we expect. That hug became a reminder that community is not accidental; it is one of God's intentional gifts. Support doesn't always come through long conversations or grand gestures--it often arrives through simple acts of kindness, offered at just the right time. God knew exactly what I needed, and He delivered it through someone willing to reach out with compassion.

Moments like these reveal how deeply God values connection. He places us among others so that we can reflect His care, encouragement, and presence to one another. Sometimes we underestimate the power of something as small as a hug, a smile, or a gentle check-in, but God uses these simple expressions to strengthen weary hearts. That Sabbath reminded me that faith is not only lived out in prayer and worship, but also in how we show up for one another.

In the stillness of that moment, I was reminded that God is always near, working quietly through the people He surrounds us with. His love is often found in the smallest gestures, wrapped in ordinary interactions that leave lasting impressions. Through that single hug, God reassured me that I was seen, supported, and held--not just by the church community, but by Him.

POEM

Joy can return in tiny moments small,
Like laughing at nothing or no reason at all.
A song in the kitchen, a dance while I clean,
Suddenly happiness sneaks on the scene.
God hides joy where I least expect it to be,
Little surprises just waiting for me.

END-OF-CHAPTER QUESTIONS

1. What small moments recently brought you unexpected joy or peace?
2. How can paying attention to simple blessings change your outlook each day?
3. What habits or thoughts sometimes prevent you from noticing joyful moments?
4. How has God encouraged you through small experiences during difficult seasons?
5. What is one simple activity you can do this week to intentionally welcome joy back into your life?

CLOSING PRAYER

Heavenly Father,

Thank You for being a God who meets us not only in life's biggest moments, but also in the smallest and quietest ones. Thank You for reminding us that Your love is never distant and never withheld, but often revealed through simple acts of kindness, gentle words, and sincere connections. We are grateful that You see every need we carry, even the ones we struggle to name, and that You care enough to meet us right where we are.

Lord, thank You for the gift of community--for the people You place in our lives to encourage us, support us, and walk alongside us. Help us never to take these blessings for granted. Teach us to recognize Your hand at work through others and to receive their care with gratitude and humility. When we feel unseen or weary, remind us that You often speak through the compassion of those around us.

Father, shape our hearts to be vessels of Your love. Make us attentive to the needs of others and sensitive to Your prompting. Help us to understand that even the smallest gestures--a kind word, a listening ear, a warm embrace--can be used by You to bring comfort and healing. May we be willing to show up for others, trusting that no act of love offered in Your name is ever wasted.

When life feels heavy or uncertain, help us to slow down and notice You in the ordinary moments. Teach us to trust that You are always working, even when Your presence feels quiet. Strengthen our faith so that we may rest in the assurance that You are near, guiding us, sustaining us, and surrounding us with Your care.

Thank You, Lord, for walking with us through every season. Thank You for reminding us that nothing in our lives is too small for Your attention or too insignificant for Your grace. As we go forward, may we carry this truth with us--that You are always present, always faithful, and always loving us through the small things.

We offer this prayer with thankful hearts, trusting You completely. In Jesus' name, Amen.

CHAPTER 12

Jesus Honors Broken Prayers

SMALL MOMENTS. BIG GOD

"Some days you don't have the words. You don't even know what to ask for. But the Spirit steps in, carrying your sighs, your heaviness, your unspoken hopes straight to the Father. Jesus honors the prayers that break apart in your hands--because He hears the heart behind them."
SCRIPTURE: Romans 8:26

FOCUS: When words fail, He still understands. Even your sighs and stumbles are carried to God with care.

Prayer does not always come out perfectly. There are times when words feel incomplete, emotions are overwhelming, or all we can offer God is silence, tears, or a simple cry for help. This message reminds us that Jesus does not require polished or perfect prayers. He understands the heart behind every word, even when we struggle to express ourselves.

Broken prayers often come from moments of deep pain, confusion, or exhaustion. During these times, honesty becomes more meaningful than eloquence. Jesus listens with compassion, recognizing the sincerity within our weakness. Even short prayers or quiet thoughts carry value because they reflect trust and openness before God.

This reflection encourages us to approach prayer without fear or pressure. We do not need the right phrases or perfect faith to be heard. Jesus honors authenticity, meeting us where we are and responding with comfort and grace. Through broken prayers, we discover that God's love reaches us most deeply when we are real and vulnerable.

And maybe I've spent too many nights trying to pray the "right" way -- trying to sound strong, steady, put-together, like I wasn't falling apart on the inside. But the truth is, some days my prayers don't come out as sentences. Some days they're just sighs. Some days they're just tears. Some days they're nothing more than a quiet, exhausted "Lord… please."

And Jesus doesn't turn away from that. He doesn't wait for me to find the perfect words or the perfect posture. He meets me right in the middle of the mess -- in the stumbles, the pauses, the trembling breaths I can't quite steady. He hears the prayers I can't finish. He understands the ones I can't explain. He carries the ones I can't even speak.

Because broken prayers aren't failures to Him. They're invitations. They're honesty. They're the kind of prayers He treasures -- the ones that come from the deepest places, the rawest places, the places I usually try to hide. Some of my prayers arrive in pieces. They don't sound like the prayers I was taught to pray or the ones I wish I knew how to offer. They come out fractured, interrupted by tears, long pauses, or the quiet admission that I don't have the words. There are moments when all I can bring to God is exhaustion and a heart that feels too heavy to explain itself.

For a long time, I wondered if those prayers mattered. I worried they were incomplete, too messy, too small. I thought prayer was supposed to be clear and confident, wrapped neatly in faith. But I've learned that the prayers that feel most broken are often the ones where God meets me most tenderly.

God has never asked me to clean up my prayers before bringing them to Him. He doesn't correct my tone or wait for me to find the right words. He listens. He stays. He meets me in the raw honesty of what I cannot fix or fully understand. And instead of repairing the prayer itself, He does something far more sacred--He begins to heal what's underneath it.

Sometimes prayer looks like sitting in silence because speaking feels like too much. Sometimes it looks like repeating the same sentence over and over, hoping it will eventually feel true. Sometimes it looks like tears falling without explanation. And still, God understands. He hears what I'm trying to say even when I can't say it. He receives what I offer, no matter how unfinished it feels.

I'm learning that broken prayers are not a sign of weak faith. They are evidence of a faith that keeps coming back, even when clarity hasn't arrived. They are proof that I still believe God is safe enough to receive me as I am. In those moments, prayer becomes less about performance and more about presence--less about saying the right thing and more about being honest enough to show up.

There is something humbling about bringing God what I don't know how to fix. About admitting that I don't have the answers, the strength, or the words. But it's in that humility that grace becomes most real. God doesn't rush me through those moments or push me toward resolution. He sits with me. He works quietly, gently reshaping my heart in ways I don't always notice right away.

I've come to see that prayer is not about impressing God or proving faith. It's about letting Him into the places that hurt the most. The places I've tried to carry alone. The places I've hidden because I didn't know how to explain them. And when I finally bring those places to Him, I discover that He has been waiting--not with judgment, but with compassion.

Broken prayers teach me that God is not intimidated by my vulnerability. He is not disappointed by my uncertainty. He is drawn to honesty, even when it comes trembling. And over time, I've noticed that while my circumstances don't always change immediately, something inside me does. My heart softens. My breathing slows. My trust deepens, not because everything makes sense, but because I am no longer carrying it alone.

So now, I bring my prayers as they are. The messy ones. The quiet ones. The ones that feel more like questions than declarations. I no longer wait until I feel strong or articulate. I come tired. I come unsure. I come exactly as I am. And every time, God meets me there--with grace that does not rush and love that does not require explanation.

If you are carrying prayers that feel broken, I hope you'll bring them too. You don't have to fix them first. You don't have to find the right words. God already knows your heart, and He is not afraid of its depth. May you find comfort in knowing that even your most fragile prayers are welcome in His presence. And may you discover that right there--in the deepest, quietest places of your heart--is where He meets you most faithfully.

TESTIMONY

The Gentle Reminder to Forgive

For a long time, I carried resentment in my heart without fully realizing how heavy it had become. What started as hurt slowly settled into something deeper, quietly affecting my thoughts, my emotions, and even my ability to experience peace. I replayed the situation over and over, holding tightly to what had wounded me, believing that my anger somehow justified the pain. Instead of protecting me, that resentment weighed on my spirit and created a distance between my heart and the peace God desired for me.

Over time, God began to gently reveal that the burden I was carrying was never meant for me to hold. He showed me that resentment was keeping me bound to the very pain I wanted to escape. Choosing forgiveness did not come easily, and it did not erase what had happened, but it marked a turning point in my heart. Forgiveness became an act of obedience and trust--a decision to place the hurt in God's hands instead of carrying it on my own.
When I finally released the resentment and chose to forgive, I felt a noticeable shift within me. The heaviness that had lingered for so long began to lift, replaced by a sense of freedom and calm I hadn't experienced in a long time. Peace slowly took the place of anger, and my heart felt lighter, no longer weighed down by bitterness. In that moment, I learned that forgiveness is not about excusing the wrong, but about allowing God to heal what resentment cannot.

That experience reminded me that freedom often begins with surrender. When we let go of what hurts us and trust God with the outcome, He restores our peace in ways we could never achieve on our own. Forgiveness opens the door for healing, and in releasing resentment, we make room for God's grace to work deeply within our hearts.

POEM

Jesus honors broken prayers I barely say right,
The ones that sound like sighs late at night.
Sometimes it's "Lord… help," nothing more,
No fancy words like I heard before.
Yet heaven listens without delay,
Understanding every messy thing I pray.

END-OF-CHAPTER QUESTIONS

1. When have you struggled to find the right words in prayer, and how did that feel?
2. How does knowing God understands your heart, even without perfect words, bring comfort?
3. What fears or doubts sometimes keep you from being honest in prayer?
4. How can simple, sincere prayers strengthen your relationship with God?
5. What is one way you can approach prayer more openly and authentically this week?

CLOSING PRAYER

Gracious and Merciful Father,

We come before You with humble hearts, thankful that You are a God who understands our pain and meets us with compassion. You see the wounds we carry, the disappointments that linger, and the resentment that quietly settles into places we try to hide. Nothing in our hearts is hidden from You, and still, You meet us with patience, love, and grace. Lord, we confess that holding onto hurt has weighed us down. We have clung to resentment thinking it would protect us, only to find it has stolen our peace and burdened our spirits. Today, we bring those heavy emotions to You. Teach us how to release what no longer serves Your purpose in our lives. Help us to trust You with the pain we cannot undo and the memories we cannot change.

Father, give us the courage to forgive--not because it is easy, but because You call us to freedom. Help us to understand that forgiveness is not about excusing the hurt or denying the impact of what was done, but about surrendering the burden into Your hands. Replace bitterness with healing, anger with peace, and heaviness with the freedom that only You can provide. Renew our hearts, Lord. Cleanse the places where resentment has taken root and restore the joy that has been diminished by unforgiveness. Teach us to walk in obedience, even when it stretches us, trusting that Your ways always lead to life and restoration. Remind us that when we forgive, we make room for Your grace to work deeply within us.

Thank You for being a God who heals what is broken and restores what feels lost. Thank You for the peace that follows surrender and the freedom that comes when we let go. As we move forward, help us to extend the same grace we have received--to others and to ourselves. May our lives reflect the mercy You have so freely given. We place our hearts in Your care, trusting You completely.

In Jesus' name, Amen.

CHAPTER 13
Letting Go Is Also Healing

SMALL MOMENTS. BIG GOD

"There's a time to hold on, and there's a time to release what's no longer serving your soul. Letting go isn't failure--it's faith. It's trusting that Jesus knows what to remove, what to restore, and what to replace. When your hands open, your heart finally has space for what He's been trying to give you."
SCRIPTURE: Ecclesiastes 3:6

FOCUS: Releasing what you can't carry anymore is part of God's timing. Letting go makes room for restoration.

Letting go can be one of the hardest parts of personal and spiritual growth. People often hold onto past hurts, disappointments, or expectations because releasing them feels uncertain or painful. This message reminds us that healing sometimes begins when we choose to release what we can no longer carry. Jesus gently teaches that freedom comes not only through holding on to faith but also through surrendering burdens to Him.

When we cling to past experiences, they can prevent us from moving forward. Letting go does not mean forgetting or pretending pain never existed; it means trusting God enough to allow restoration to take place. Through forgiveness, acceptance, and trust, space is created for peace to grow.

This reflection encourages courage in the process of release. Jesus walks with us as we loosen our grip on fear, regret, or control, replacing heaviness with renewal. By letting go, we open our hearts to healing and discover that God often brings new strength and clarity when we trust Him with what we release.

And maybe I held on longer than I should have. Not because it was healthy, but because it was familiar. Because letting go felt like losing, and losing felt like failing. But God keeps reminding me that release is not defeat -- it's deliverance.

Some things can't go with me into the next season. Some weights were never mine to carry. Some people were only meant to walk with me for a chapter, not the whole story. And the longer I cling to what's slipping away, the more I delay what God is trying to place in my hands.

Letting go doesn't mean I didn't love well. It doesn't mean I didn't try. It doesn't mean the past wasn't real or meaningful. It simply means I'm choosing healing over holding on to what hurts. And healing often begins with release -- the quiet kind, the painful kind, the kind that feels like breaking but is actually making room. Room for peace. Room for clarity. Room for the version of me God is shaping next. Letting go has taught me more about trust than holding on ever did. It asks me to loosen my grip on what feels familiar, even when it's painful, and place it in God's care instead. This kind of release isn't passive or careless--it's intentional. It's choosing to believe that God's timing is wiser than mine, that His plans reach further than what I can see, and that His heart toward me is always good, even when I don't understand the path ahead.

Letting go doesn't mean pretending something didn't matter or erasing what shaped me. It doesn't ask me to forget the love, the loss, or the lessons. It simply asks me to stop carrying the weight of what was never meant to rest solely on my shoulders. Surrender is not denial--it's trust placed in the right hands.

Sometimes letting go feels like releasing expectations I've clung to too tightly. Other times it looks like handing God my unanswered questions, my timelines, and the outcomes I've rehearsed a thousand times in my mind. It's admitting that control has never actually been mine, and that peace doesn't come from holding everything together, but from trusting the One who already is.

There are days when surrender feels gentle, and days when it feels like a deep ache. But even then, I'm learning that God is careful with what I give Him. He does not mishandle my story. He does not waste what I release. What feels uncertain to me is already known to Him.

Letting go becomes an act of faith each time I choose trust over fear. Each time I place my future--unfinished and unclear--into God's care. And while I may not know what comes next, I'm learning to believe that the One who holds tomorrow is worthy of my trust today.

So, I end this chapter with this truth resting gently in my spirit: Letting go is not weakness. Letting go is not quitting. Letting go is also healing -- and sometimes, it's the bravest thing I'll ever do.

TESTIMONY

The Helpful Neighbor

There was a time when a neighbor noticed a small need I had and offered to help without hesitation. It wasn't anything major--just a simple act--but it came at a moment when I felt overwhelmed and could truly use the support. That small gesture made a bigger impact than they probably realized. In that moment, I was reminded that I didn't have to carry everything by myself.

Their kindness stayed with me because it reflected something deeper than just helpfulness. It revealed the quiet way God often cares for us through the people He places in our lives. Sometimes help comes not in the form of dramatic answers or big solutions, but through someone willing to step in and lend a hand in ordinary circumstances. That simple act reminded me that we are meant to look out for one another and share one another's burdens.

God designed us for connection, not isolation. When we choose to help, encourage, or support someone--even in small ways--we become part of how God shows His love. That moment with my neighbor reminded me that kindness is never wasted. Even the smallest acts of support can speak loudly to a weary heart and serve as a gentle reminder that we are seen, valued, and cared for by God through one another.

POEM

Letting go is healing, though I hold on tight,
Replaying old stories every single night.
God says, "Release it," and I argue back,
Like peace might disappear if I loosen my grip's track.
But freedom shows up when I finally yield,
And open hands become a healed field.

END-OF-CHAPTER QUESTIONS

1. What situation, memory, or expectation might you need to release in order to move forward?
2. Why can letting go sometimes feel more difficult than holding on?
3. How has holding onto past pain affected your peace or growth?
4. What does trusting God look like when you choose to release control?
5. What is one small step you can take toward emotional or spiritual freedom this week?

CLOSING PRAYER

Loving and Faithful God,

Thank You for being a God who sees every detail of our lives and meets us through moments that often seem ordinary. Thank You for the quiet ways You show Your care--through helping hands, thoughtful gestures, and people who step in at just the right time. We are grateful that You remind us, again and again, that we are not meant to walk through life alone.

Lord, thank You for the gift of community and for the neighbors, friends, and strangers You use to reflect Your love. Help us to recognize these moments for what they are--divine reminders of Your presence and provision. When someone offers help, encouragement, or kindness, open our hearts to receive it with gratitude and humility, knowing that You are often working through others to meet our needs.

Father, shape our hearts to be attentive and willing. Teach us not to overlook small opportunities to serve, to help, or to show compassion. Remind us that even the simplest acts--lending a hand, offering time, noticing a need--can carry great meaning when done in love. May we never underestimate how You can use our obedience in small things to bring comfort and hope to someone else.

When we feel overwhelmed or stretched thin, help us to trust that You will provide support in ways we may not expect. Give us eyes to see Your grace at work around us and hearts that remain open to connection. Guard us from pride or isolation, and help us lean into the relationships You place in our lives.

Lord, let our lives be a reflection of Your kindness. As You care for us through others, teach us to do the same. May we be known as people who uplift, encourage, and support those around us--not for recognition, but out of love and obedience to You. Use our everyday actions to reveal Your goodness and remind others that they are seen and valued.

Thank You for walking with us in both the big moments and the small ones. Thank You for showing us that nothing done in love is ever insignificant. We place our trust in You, confident that You are always at work, weaving Your grace through the ordinary details of our lives.

We offer this prayer with thankful hearts,
In Jesus' name, Amen.

CHAPTER 14
Jesus Rebuilds Confidence Gradually

SMALL MOMENTS. BIG GOD

"We overlook the beginnings--the tiny steps, the quiet progress, the almost-nothing moments. But God doesn't. He celebrates what we call small because He sees what it's becoming. Jesus builds big things out of little faith, little efforts, little yeses. Nothing is insignificant when He's in it."
SCRIPTURE: Zechariah 4:10

FOCUS: He starts with small beginnings, steady steps, and quiet progress--teaching you to trust the growth you can't always see.

Confidence can be shaken by failure, disappointment, or difficult life experiences. When trust in us is damaged, it often takes time to feel strong again. This message reminds us that Jesus restores confidence slowly and patiently, helping us rebuild belief in who we are and what we are capable of becoming.

Rather than changing everything at once, Jesus works through small successes and everyday lessons. Each step forward, no matter how small, becomes part of the rebuilding process. Moments of courage, learning from mistakes, and choosing to try again help restore inner strength little by little. Over time, fear begins to lose its control as faith grows stronger.

This reflection encourages patience with personal growth. Confidence is not rebuilt through perfection but through consistent progress and trust in God's guidance. As Jesus strengthens us gradually, we begin to see ourselves through His perspective -- valued, capable, and supported -- learning that true confidence is rooted in faith rather than circumstances. And maybe confidence doesn't return all at once. Maybe it doesn't rush back in with fireworks or loud announcements. Sometimes it tiptoes. Sometimes it rebuilds itself in whispers -- in small wins, quiet reminders, and moments I almost miss because they don't feel big enough to matter. But Jesus sees every inch of progress.

He celebrates the days I stand a little taller, even if I still feel shaky. He honors the moments I try again after failing, the moments I speak up after shrinking back, the moments I choose courage even when fear is still sitting in the room. He doesn't shame me for losing confidence. He doesn't rush me to recover it. He rebuilds it with patience -- brick by brick, truth by truth, step by step. He reminds me who I am in Him until I start to believe it again. And even when

I don't feel bold, He calls me brave. Even when I feel small, He calls me chosen. Even when I feel unsure, He calls me His. I'm learning that confidence doesn't mean the absence of questions or fear. It doesn't arrive because doubt has finally disappeared. More often, it shows up right in the middle of uncertainty--when I don't have clear answers and still feel unsure of my footing. Confidence, for me, has become less about feeling certain and more about recognizing God's voice when everything else feels unsettled.

Doubt still visits. It still whispers questions and points out what I don't know. But I'm discovering that God doesn't withdraw when doubt appears. He steps closer. His voice becomes an anchor--quiet, steady, and reassuring--reminding me of what is true when my thoughts begin to spiral. Confidence grows not because the questions are gone, but because His presence is stronger than them. God doesn't rebuild confidence quickly or carelessly. He restores it slowly, layer by layer, with patience and intention. He allows it to form in real places--in lived experience, in answered prayers, in moments of endurance I didn't think I had. What He builds isn't fragile or forced. It's rooted. And because it takes time, it lasts.

There are seasons when confidence feels small and tentative, when it looks more like trust than boldness. But even then, God is at work. He's teaching me to listen for His voice above my fears, to believe what He says over what doubt insists on repeating. Confidence becomes less about self-assurance and more about dependence--resting in the truth that God is near and faithful.

Over time, I'm learning that the confidence God gives is not loud or flashy. It doesn't rush ahead or pretend certainty where there is none. It stands quietly in the presence of doubt and chooses to trust anyway. And that kind of confidence--built slowly, shaped by grace, and anchored in God's voice--is strong enough to remain, even when the questions return.

So, I end this chapter with this truth resting deep in my spirit: Confidence doesn't have to come back quickly to be real. It doesn't have to be loud to be strong. Jesus rebuilds confidence gradually -- and every slow, steady piece He restores is shaping me into someone who can stand again, speak again, and believe again. And somehow, that gradual rebuilding becomes the most lasting kind of confidence of all.

TESTIMONY

The Peaceful Prayer

There was a moment when my heart felt restless and burdened, weighed down by thoughts I couldn't quiet on my own. I carried concerns into the day and into the night, trying to reason through them, yet finding no relief. In that place of heaviness, I turned to prayer--not with eloquent words or great expectations, but simply with honesty and a desire for peace.

As I began to pray, something gentle yet profound took place. I didn't receive immediate answers, and nothing around me changed outwardly, but something within me began to settle. The noise in my thoughts softened, and the tension I had been holding slowly loosened its grip. In that quiet moment with God, I felt His presence surround me with calm and reassurance.

That prayer reminded me that peace does not always come from solutions or understanding, but from surrender. As I placed my worries into God's hands, I felt a sense of rest replace the anxiety I had been carrying. It was as though God was reminding me that I didn't have to have everything figured out--I simply needed to trust Him with what I could not control.

What stayed with me most was the stillness that followed. My circumstances remained the same, yet my heart felt lighter. That peaceful prayer became a reminder that God meets us in our vulnerability and offers comfort that goes beyond words. He listens when we come to Him honestly, and He responds with a peace that quiets the soul.

Through that experience, I was reminded that prayer is not about perfection--it is about connection. In those moments when we pause, breathe, and place our trust in God, He faithfully meets us with His presence. That peaceful prayer taught me that even in the midst of uncertainty, God is near, offering rest, clarity, and peace that carries us forward.

POEM

Jesus rebuilds confidence slowly, piece by piece,
Not overnight magic, but growing inner peace.
I fall, get up, then trip once more,
Yet He still cheers louder than before.
Step by step my courage learns to stand,
As faith rewrites the doubts I planned.

END-OF-CHAPTER QUESTIONS

1. What experiences have affected your confidence, either positively or negatively?
2. How have small successes helped you regain trust in yourself over time?
3. In what ways can patience support your personal and spiritual growth?
4. How does relying on God's guidance help rebuild confidence after setbacks?
5. What is one small step you can take this week to strengthen your confidence and move forward?

CLOSING PRAYER

Heavenly Father,
We come before You with grateful hearts, thankful for the peace You offer so freely when we come to You in prayer. Thank You for being a God who listens patiently, even when our words are few and our hearts feel heavy. In Your presence, we find rest for our souls and reassurance that we are never alone.

Lord, thank You for the stillness You bring when our minds are overwhelmed and our spirits feel unsettled. Thank You for reminding us that we do not need to have all the answers before we come to You. You invite us just as we are--with our worries, uncertainties, and unspoken fears--and You meet us with calm, understanding, and grace.

Father, help us to remember that prayer is not about perfect words, but about sincere connection. Teach us to pause, to breathe, and to place our trust fully in You. When anxiety rises and peace feels distant, gently draw us back into moments of quiet surrender. Remind us that Your peace does not depend on changing circumstances, but on trusting Your presence within them.

Fill our hearts with the peace that only You can give--the kind that settles our thoughts, softens our worries, and strengthens our faith. Help us to carry that peace with us into our daily lives, allowing it to guide our decisions, our responses, and our relationships. May it overflow into how we speak, how we listen, and how we love others.

Lord, when life feels noisy and demanding, teach us to return often to prayer as a place of refuge. Help us to recognize those sacred moments when You calm our spirits and remind us that You are in control. May we never underestimate the power of a quiet prayer offered in faith.

Thank You for walking with us through every season and for meeting us in both the stillness and the uncertainty. We trust You with what we cannot change and rest in the peace You provide. As we move forward, may our hearts remain anchored in You, confident that Your presence is always near.

We surrender all to You with thankful hearts.
In Jesus' name, Amen.

CHAPTER 15
Jesus Is in Daily Decisions

SMALL MOMENTS. BIG GOD

"You don't have to figure everything out. God never asked you to. He simply invites you to trust Him with the pieces that don't make sense and the paths that aren't clear. When you lean on Jesus instead of your own understanding, He doesn't just guide your steps--He straightens the road beneath your feet."
SCRIPTURE: Proverbs 3:5-6

FOCUS: When I trust Him with the small choices, He guides my steps and makes the path clear.

Faith is often connected to big life choices, but many of the most important spiritual moments happen through everyday decisions. This message reminds us that Jesus is present not only during major turning points but also in the small choices we make each day. How we speak to others, how we respond to challenges, and how we manage our attitudes all reflect our spiritual journey.

Daily decisions shape character over time. Choosing patience instead of anger, honesty instead of convenience, or compassion instead of judgment allows faith to become part of ordinary living. Jesus guides us through quiet nudges, wisdom, and moments of reflection that help us move in healthier and more loving directions. This reflection encourages awareness and intentional living. When we invite Jesus into our everyday choices, even routine moments gain deeper meaning. By trusting Him in small decisions, we grow spiritually and learn that faith is not separate from daily life but woven into every step we take.

And maybe I used to think Jesus only showed up in the big choices -- the life-changing moments, the crossroads, the situations that felt too heavy for me to handle alone. But the more I walk with Him, the more I realize He's just as present in the small decisions that shape my day. He's in the moment I choose patience instead of snapping back. He's in the quiet nudge that tells me to pause before I speak. He's in the strength it takes to walk away from what drains me and lean toward what brings peace. He's in the wisdom that whispers, "Not that way… this way." He's in the courage to say yes, and the clarity to say no.

Jesus doesn't wait for the dramatic moments to guide me -- He's in the ordinary ones, the overlooked ones, the ones I make without thinking. He's teaching me that faith isn't just about trusting Him with my future; it's about trusting Him with my next step, my next thought, my next choice. I'm learning that God is not only present in the big, defining moments of life, but deeply involved in the ordinary ones too. He meets me in the routines I barely notice, the quiet pauses between responsibilities, and the small decisions that seem insignificant at the time. These everyday moments are where my heart is slowly shaped, where faith becomes lived rather than spoken.

God is near in the choices I make when no one else is watching--in how I respond instead of react, how I choose grace over frustration, how I show up even when I feel tired or unsure. These small decisions may not feel spiritual or important, but they are often where obedience takes root and trust grows. They are the places where love becomes tangible.

I'm realizing that God doesn't rush me past the ordinary. He works within it. He uses the unnoticed moments to draw me closer, to teach me to listen, to invite me into a deeper awareness of His presence. When I slow down enough to notice Him there, even the simplest parts of my day become sacred.

So I'm learning to pay attention--to look for Him in my daily choices, in the quiet faithfulness of showing up again and again. And I'm discovering that when I do, those small steps gently lead me closer to Him, shaping my heart in ways I couldn't have planned on my own.

May you come to recognize God's nearness in the everyday moments of your life. May you see His hand in your daily choices, and may each one--no matter how small--draw you closer to Him.

So, I end this chapter with this truth settled deep in my spirit: Jesus is not just the God of big decisions -- He's the God of daily ones. And when I invite Him into the small choices, I look back and realize He's been shaping my whole life one quiet decision at a time.

TESTIMONY

The End of the Day Reflection

As the day came to an end and everything finally grew quiet, I took time to reflect on the moments I had almost overlooked. That was when I realized how faithfully Jesus had been present with me throughout the day. Not in ways that demanded attention or stood out as extraordinary, but in small, meaningful moments that gently touched my heart. His presence was there in a kind conversation that brought encouragement when I needed it, in a peaceful thought that calmed my mind when it felt unsettled, and in a quiet prayer that rose naturally from a place of trust rather than urgency.

Looking back, I understood that those moments were not random or insignificant. They were reminders that Jesus walks with us through the ordinary rhythms of our lives, meeting us in ways that feel personal and intentional. He didn't wait for the day to be perfect or for me to be fully aware; He was already there, offering reassurance, peace, and companionship in subtle ways. It was only when I slowed down that I began to recognize how gently He had been guiding my thoughts and steadying my spirit.

That realization shifted my perspective. What once felt like just another routine day became a collection of sacred moments woven together by His presence. I was reminded that Jesus often speaks through simplicity--through calm thoughts, quiet prayers, and ordinary interactions that carry deeper meaning. When we pause to reflect, we begin to see that He is always near, faithfully present in the small details of our lives, reminding us that nothing is too small to be touched by His love.

POEM

Jesus is in daily decisions, big and small,
Like "Should I respond… or not text back at all?"
In coffee choices and paths I choose,
Guiding my steps so I don't always lose.
Even simple moments become precision,
When faith helps shape each daily decision.

END-OF-CHAPTER QUESTIONS

1. What small daily choices have the greatest impact on your attitude or direction in life?
2. How can you become more mindful of God's guidance when making everyday decisions?
3. When have you felt peace after choosing what you believed was the right path?
4. What habits can help you pause and reflect before making important choices?
5. What is one decision this week where you can intentionally seek wisdom and prayer first?

CLOSING PRAYER

Dear Jesus,
As this day comes to an end, we pause to thank You for Your faithful presence in every moment--both the ones we noticed and the ones we almost overlooked. Thank You for walking with us through the ordinary rhythms of our lives, reminding us that You are near even when life feels quiet and routine. We are grateful that You do not limit Your presence to grand moments, but lovingly meet us in the small details of each day.

Lord, thank You for the gentle ways You reveal Yourself to us. Thank You for kind conversations that bring encouragement, for peaceful thoughts that calm our hearts, and for quiet prayers that draw us closer to You. Help us to recognize these moments as sacred, knowing that they are evidence of Your care and attentiveness. Teach us to slow down and become more aware of how often You are at work around us.

Father, forgive us for the times we rush through our days and miss Your presence. Open our eyes to see You more clearly and our hearts to feel You more deeply. Help us to develop a spirit of gratitude, one that recognizes Your hand not only in answered prayers, but also in moments of stillness, reassurance, and peace. May we learn to treasure the small ways You guide us and trust that You are always with us.

Jesus, we invite Your peace to settle over us tonight. Quiet our thoughts, calm our spirits, and help us release anything we are carrying that does not belong to us. Teach us to rest in You, confident that You hold every detail of our lives. Remind us that we do not need to strive or worry, because You are already present, already working, already faithful.

As we move forward, help us to live with greater awareness of Your nearness. May our hearts remain attentive to Your voice, our minds open to Your guidance, and our lives shaped by gratitude for Your constant companionship. Let our days be marked not by busyness, but by a growing recognition of Your love woven into every moment.

Thank You, Jesus, for meeting us in the small things. Thank You for walking with us when no one else sees. We trust You completely and rest in the assurance that You are always near.

We offer this prayer with thankful hearts, in Your precious name, Amen.

CHAPTER 16

Jesus Works Through Routine

SMALL MOMENTS. BIG GOD

"Whatever you're doing--big task or small chore--Jesus sees the heart behind it. When you give your best, not for applause but for Him, the ordinary becomes holy. Even the unnoticed work matters when it's done with devotion."
SCRIPTURE: Colossians 3:23

FOCUS: Even the everyday tasks matter to Him. When I do them with heart, He turns routine into worship.

Routines can sometimes feel boring or repetitive, making life seem ordinary and predictable. However, this message reminds us that Jesus often works through the very routines we overlook. Daily habits such as working, caring for family, completing responsibilities, and maintaining simple schedules create opportunities for growth, discipline, and spiritual awareness.

Instead of waiting for something exciting to happen, we begin to see that consistency itself has value. Through routine, Jesus teaches patience, responsibility, and faithfulness. Small repeated actions -- showing kindness, staying committed, and doing our best even when no one notices -- help shape character over time. These steady moments become the foundation for deeper spiritual strength. This reflection encourages us to appreciate everyday rhythms rather than resist them. When we invite Jesus into our routines, ordinary tasks gain purpose and meaning. What once felt repetitive becomes a place where faith is practiced daily, reminding us that God is present not only in change but also in the steady flow of everyday life. And maybe I used to overlook the ordinary -- the small tasks, the repeated rhythms, the parts of my day that felt too simple to matter. But the more I walk with Jesus, the more I realize He's been moving in those places all along. He's in the way I start my morning, even when I'm tired. He's in the chores I rush through, the errands I don't enjoy, the responsibilities that feel endless. He's in the conversations I didn't plan, the moments of patience I didn't think I had, the tiny choices that shape who I'm becoming. Jesus doesn't wait for a big moment to show up -- He steps into the routine, the repetitive, the predictable. He turns the everyday into evidence of His presence. He uses the ordinary to grow me in ways I don't notice until later. Because routine isn't wasted. Routine is where character is formed. Routine is where faith becomes muscle. Routine is where obedience becomes lifestyle. I'm learning that

God is not only present in the moments that feel meaningful or significant, but deeply involved in the ordinary patterns of my days. He meets me in the routines I move through almost on autopilot--the familiar rhythms, the repeated tasks, the small choices that don't feel spiritual at all. And yet, these are often the very places where my heart is being shaped the most.

God is near in the everyday moments I'm tempted to rush past. He's present in how I begin my mornings, how I respond when I'm tired, how I choose patience when irritation would be easier. The small decisions I make--how I speak, how I listen, how I show kindness or extend grace--quietly form who I'm becoming. They don't feel dramatic, but they matter deeply.

I'm discovering that purpose isn't reserved for big callings or life-changing events. It's woven into the ordinary. God uses the steady rhythms of daily life to draw me closer to Him, teaching me faithfulness through consistency and trust through repetition. When I slow down enough to notice Him there, the mundane becomes meaningful.

There are days when nothing feels extraordinary, when life is made up of responsibilities and routines. But even then, God is present. He is not waiting for me to arrive at something bigger before He meets me. He is already here, inviting me to recognize Him in every part of my day.

May you begin to see the ordinary through new eyes. May you find purpose in the routines you walk through and meaning in the rhythms you live within. And may you recognize God's presence in every small choice you make, trusting that even the simplest moments can gently lead you closer to Him.

So, I end this chapter with this truth settled deep in my spirit: Jesus isn't just in the miracles -- He's in the Monday mornings. He's in the dishes, the commutes, the conversations. He's in the quiet habits that shape my heart when no one is watching. Jesus works through routine -- and when I look back, I realize He's been using the smallest parts of my day to build the biggest parts of my life.

TESTIMONY

The Encouraging Text

One morning, someone unexpectedly came to mind. There was no clear reason or recent conversation--just a quiet thought that lingered. Instead of brushing it aside, I felt prompted to reach out. I sent a brief message letting them know they were on my heart and that I was praying for them. It took only a few moments, and at the time, it felt like a simple, ordinary act.

Later that day, I heard back from them, and what they shared stayed with me. They explained that the day had been especially heavy and discouraging, and the message arrived at a moment when they truly needed reassurance. Those few words of encouragement reminded them that they weren't alone and that someone cared. Hearing that made me pause and reflect.

That experience reminded me how often Jesus works through small, quiet acts of obedience. What felt insignificant to me became meaningful to someone else because God was in it. Jesus didn't need a long conversation or a grand gesture to bring comfort--He moved through a simple message, sent at just the right time.

It taught me the importance of paying attention to those gentle nudges and responding with faith, even when the action seems small. Sometimes Jesus chooses to reach hearts through our willingness to act, reminding us that even the simplest expressions of care can carry His love and encouragement exactly where it's needed.

POEM

Jesus works through routine, the same old day,
While I'm brushing my teeth half-asleep, trying to pray.
In morning alarms and chores I repeat,
He turns ordinary rhythms into something sweet.
Not every miracle comes with a boom,
Sometimes it shows up while I clean my room.

END-OF-CHAPTER QUESTIONS

1. Which daily routines in your life feel ordinary but may hold deeper purpose?
2. How can consistency in small habits strengthen your faith over time?
3. What attitude changes could help you see routine tasks as meaningful instead of repetitive?
4. How has God helped you grow through responsibilities you repeat each day?
5. What is one routine you can approach differently this week by inviting God into it?

CLOSING PRAYER

Gracious and Loving Father,
Thank You for being a God who speaks in gentle ways and invites us to listen with open hearts. Thank You for the quiet nudges You place within us--the moments when You bring someone to mind and call us to act in love. We are grateful that You choose to work through ordinary people and simple acts, using them to bring encouragement, comfort, and hope to others.

Lord, teach us to be attentive to Your voice. Help us not to ignore or dismiss the small promptings You place on our hearts. Give us the willingness to obey, even when the action feels insignificant or inconvenient. Remind us that obedience does not always require grand gestures; often it begins with a simple step taken in faith--a message sent, a prayer offered, or a word of encouragement shared. Father, give us hearts that are sensitive to the needs of others. Help us to recognize that You may be inviting us to be an answer to someone else's prayer. When You lead us to reach out, grant us courage and compassion, trusting that You will use our obedience in ways we may never fully see. Teach us to trust that no act done in love is ever wasted.

Thank You, Lord, for showing us that encouragement can arrive at just the right moment and that You are always working behind the scenes. When we choose to respond to You, You multiply what we offer and use it to strengthen weary hearts. Help us to walk daily with a spirit of availability, ready to be used by You however You choose.

As we go forward, help us to remain faithful in small things. May our lives reflect a quiet obedience that honors You and a willingness to encourage others as You lead. Keep us humble, attentive, and responsive to Your guidance. Let our actions point others to Your love and remind them that they are not alone.

We place our trust in You, grateful that You are always at work through the simplest acts of faith. Thank You for inviting us to partner with You in bringing light, hope, and encouragement into the lives of others.

We offer this prayer with grateful hearts,
In Jesus' name, Amen.

CHAPTER 17
Jesus Is Present in Work and Responsibility

SMALL MOMENTS. BIG GOD

"Whatever your hands find to do, do it with intention. Not perfection, not pressure--just wholehearted effort. Jesus meets you in the work right in front of you, turning ordinary tasks into meaningful offerings. When you give your best where you are, He breathes purpose into what might seem small."
SCRIPTURE: Ecclesiastes 9:10

FOCUS: When I give my best to what's in front of me, He meets me there. Even ordinary work becomes sacred when He's in it.

Work and responsibility are often viewed as separate from spiritual life, but this message reminds us that Jesus is present in the tasks and duties we carry each day. Whether at a job, caring for family, managing a home, or fulfilling commitments, these responsibilities become meaningful when approached with faith and purpose.

Daily work can feel tiring or routine, yet it provides opportunities to practice patience, integrity, and dedication. Jesus strengthens us through effort, teaching us to serve others with humility and to find value in doing even small tasks well. Responsibility becomes more than obligation; it becomes a way of expressing gratitude and stewardship for what God has entrusted to us.

This reflection encourages us to see work as part of our spiritual journey rather than a distraction from it. When we invite Jesus into our responsibilities, ordinary labor gains deeper meaning. Through faithful effort and honest service, we discover that God's presence is not limited to moments of prayer but is active in the work of everyday life.

And maybe I used to think God only moved in the spiritual moments -- the worship, the prayer, the quiet time, the places where my hands were lifted instead of busy. But the more life stretches me, the more I realize He's just as present in the work I do with tired hands and a full schedule. He's there when I show up even though I'm overwhelmed. He's there when I handle responsibilities no one sees or thanks me for. He's there in the decisions I make, the tasks I juggle, the strength I borrow just to get through the day. He's there in the discipline, the diligence, the effort that feels ordinary but matters more than I know.

Jesus doesn't step back when life gets practical. He doesn't disappear when the to-do list grows. He walks with me into every meeting, every chore, every assignment, every obligation. He turns my work into worship, my responsibility into purpose, my effort into offering. And even when I feel stretched thin, He reminds me that I'm not carrying any of it alone. He gives wisdom when I'm unsure, peace when I'm pressured, and strength when I'm spent. He honors the work I do quietly, faithfully, consistently -- the kind of work that shapes character and builds endurance. I'm learning that God is not only present in the moments that feel meaningful or visible, but deeply involved in the everyday grind--the work no one applauds, the responsibilities that feel repetitive, the effort that goes unnoticed. He meets me in the hidden labor of ordinary days, in the tasks that don't feel spiritual but require faithfulness all the same. These are the places where endurance is formed and character is shaped.

God is present in the work I do when I'm tired, when motivation is thin, and when the results feel slow or invisible. He sees the faithfulness it takes to keep showing up, to keep caring, to keep carrying what has been entrusted to me. Even when my work feels small or overlooked, it is not meaningless to Him. Nothing done with sincerity and obedience is ever wasted in His hands.

I'm beginning to understand that purpose isn't always found in passion or big moments--it's often found in perseverance. In choosing to do the next right thing. In being faithful with what's in front of me today. God works quietly through consistency, shaping my heart in the rhythm of responsibility and teaching me to trust Him in the ordinary flow of life.

The everyday grind can feel heavy, but God is there too. He brings meaning to the mundane and dignity to the unseen work. He reminds me that faithfulness is not glamorous, but it is powerful. It is often in the hidden places that trust grows deepest and reliance on Him becomes most real.

May you begin to see your work through God's eyes--not as something to simply get through, but as a place where He is near and actively present. May you find purpose in the responsibilities you carry, even when they feel heavy or repetitive. And may you recognize that God is with you in every effort, every task, every quiet act of faithfulness--working in you and through you, even when no one else sees.

So, I end this chapter with this truth settled deep in my spirit: Jesus is not distant from my daily grind. He is present in it -- guiding, strengthening, steadying, and reminding me that what I do matters. My work is not wasted. My responsibility is not unnoticed. And with Him beside me, even the ordinary becomes holy.

TESTIMONY

The Grocery Line

I was standing in a long grocery line when an unexpected moment unfolded in front of me. The woman ahead of me suddenly realized she didn't have enough money to cover all the items she had gathered. I could see the discomfort wash over her face as she looked down, trying to decide what to remove. Her embarrassment was quiet but obvious, and the moment felt heavy with unspoken emotion.

Without drawing attention to the situation, I quietly stepped in and paid the small amount she was short. It wasn't something I planned or thought through--it was simply a response in the moment. When she realized what had happened, she turned toward me with a smile filled with gratitude, her eyes welling with tears. No long conversation was needed; the exchange itself spoke volumes.

As I walked away, my heart felt deeply stirred. That simple act reminded me how much kindness matters, especially when it preserves someone's dignity. What felt small to me carried great meaning for her, and in that quiet moment, I sensed Jesus gently reminding me that love is often expressed through ordinary opportunities.

That experience stayed with me because it revealed how present Jesus is in everyday life. He often invites us to act with compassion in simple, unnoticed ways. In that grocery store line, I was reminded that even the smallest acts of kindness can become reflections of

His love, touching hearts and leaving lasting impressions far beyond the moment itself.

POEM

Jesus is present in work and responsibility too,
Even when my to-do list multiplies out of the blue.
In emails, deadlines, and bills to pay,
He walks beside me through the busy day.
Holiness isn't just prayer on display,
It's faith showing up while I earn my way.

END-OF-CHAPTER QUESTIONS

1. How can you view your daily work or responsibilities as part of your spiritual journey?
2. What challenges at work or at home test your patience or character the most?
3. In what ways can honesty and dedication reflect your faith in everyday tasks?
4. How has God strengthened you during seasons of heavy responsibility?
5. What is one practical way you can invite God's presence into your work this week?

CLOSING PRAYER

Loving and Compassionate Father,
We thank You for being a God who notices every detail and cares deeply about the quiet moments of our lives. Thank You for reminding us that kindness matters and that even the smallest acts, when done in love, can reflect Your heart in powerful ways. You see the needs that go unnoticed by others, and You invite us to be vessels of Your compassion in everyday situations.

Lord, thank You for the opportunities You place before us to show kindness, often when we least expect them. Help us to be attentive to those moments and willing to respond with humility and grace. Teach us to see people through Your eyes, especially when they feel vulnerable, embarrassed, or unseen. May we never overlook the chance to preserve someone's dignity through quiet generosity and sincere care.

Father, shape our hearts to be generous--not only with what we have, but with compassion, patience, and understanding. Remind us that giving does not always require much; sometimes it simply requires obedience and a willing heart. Help us to trust that when we act in love, You will use even our smallest offerings to bring encouragement and hope to others.

Jesus, thank You for walking with us through ordinary places and moments--through grocery stores, lines, and simple encounters where Your love can be revealed. Help us to recognize that You are present in these moments, gently reminding us that our actions can reflect Your kindness more clearly than words ever could. Let our lives quietly point others to You.

As we go forward, help us to remain sensitive to Your leading. Give us courage to act when You prompt us and humility to serve without seeking recognition. May our kindness be sincere, our generosity thoughtful, and our hearts always open to Your guidance.

Thank You for reminding us that love lived out in small ways still carries eternal value. We place our trust in You, confident that You are always working through simple acts of obedience to touch lives and reveal Your grace.

We offer this prayer with grateful hearts,
In Jesus' name, Amen.

CHAPTER 18

Jesus Uses Waiting Seasons

SMALL MOMENTS. BIG GOD

"God isn't slow--He's intentional. While you're waiting for answers, He's waiting to be gracious. His timing isn't a delay but a doorway, opening at the exact moment mercy will mean the most. Jesus doesn't rush your story; He stays with you in the in-between, turning waiting into a place where trust grows." SCRIPTURE: Isaiah 30:18

FOCUS: Delays aren't punishment--they're preparation. In the waiting, He shapes your strength and deepens your trust.

Waiting can feel frustrating, especially when we are ready for change or hoping for answers. Seasons of delay often make people feel stuck or forgotten. This message reminds us that waiting is not wasted time. Jesus uses these periods to prepare our hearts, strengthen our faith, and help us grow in ways we may not immediately understand.

During waiting seasons, patience is developed and perspective begins to change. We learn to trust God's timing rather than rushing ahead on our own plans. Even when nothing seems to be happening on the surface, important inner work is taking place -- shaping character, building resilience, and teaching reliance on God instead of circumstances.

This reflection encourages us to view waiting differently. Instead of seeing it as a pause in progress, we can recognize it as part of the journey. Jesus remains active during these quiet seasons, guiding and preparing us for what lies ahead. In time, we often realize that waiting helped us become ready for the blessings and responsibilities that followed. And maybe waiting has never felt natural to me. I'm wired to move, to fix, to figure things out, to make something happen. But waiting? Waiting feels like standing still while life keeps running ahead without me. It feels like silence where I wanted answers, delay where I wanted direction, and uncertainty where I wanted clarity. But Jesus keeps teaching me that waiting is not wasted. It's not punishment. It's not abandonment. It's preparation.

In the waiting, He slows me down long enough to heal what I ignored. He strengthens what was weak, restores what was broken, and reveals what I couldn't see when I was rushing. He grows roots in me -- deep ones -- the kind that can only form when life isn't moving at my preferred speed. And even when I feel stuck, He's not still. He's working behind the scenes, aligning what I can't see, protecting me from what I don't know, and shaping me for what's ahead. Waiting seasons become holy ground when I realize He's using them to build the version of me that the next season will require. Waiting has become one of my greatest teachers, even though it's never been my favorite place to be. It stretches me in ways I didn't ask for and exposes how much I want clarity before I'm ready to trust. But I'm learning that waiting is not wasted time. It's the space where God's timing gently meets my readiness--where He works in me before He works around me.

When I'm waiting, it often feels like nothing is happening. Days pass, prayers feel unanswered, and progress seems invisible. But beneath the surface, God is doing something deeper than I can see. He is shaping my heart, softening my expectations, strengthening my faith, and preparing me for what's coming next--long before I realize I need that preparation.

Waiting teaches me that readiness isn't about having everything figured out. It's about becoming someone who can receive what God wants to give without fear or striving. Sometimes the delay isn't punishment or neglect--it's protection. God knows what I'm not yet ready to carry, and He loves me enough to prepare me slowly.

There are moments when waiting feels lonely, when I wonder if I've been forgotten or left behind. But even there, God is present. He's attentive in the silence, intentional in the stillness. He's working in the unseen places--aligning timing, healing wounds, deepening trust--long before anything changes on the outside.

I'm learning that waiting doesn't mean God is holding back. It means He's holding me. Teaching me patience. Teaching me dependence. Teaching me to trust His heart even when I don't understand His pace. And when the next step finally comes, I'll realize that the waiting was part of the gift--it prepared me to step forward with faith instead of fear.

So I'm learning to wait with open hands instead of clenched fists. To trust that God sees the full picture, even when I only see today. And to believe that He is preparing me for what's next, even now, even here--even when I don't yet understand what that will be.

So, I end this chapter with this truth resting gently in my spirit: Waiting is not a pause in God's plan -- it's part of it. It's where He prepares me, grows me, steadies me, and reminds me that His timing is not a threat to my future but a safeguard for it. Jesus uses waiting seasons -- and when I finally step into what He's been preparing, I'll see that the waiting was working all along.

TESTIMONY

The Parking Spot

I was driving slowly through a busy parking lot, turning down one row and then another, scanning for any sign of an open space. Cars were packed tightly together, and it seemed as though everyone had arrived at the same time. After a few laps, I felt that familiar mix of impatience and mild frustration creeping in. I wasn't in a crisis. I wasn't facing anything dramatic or life-altering. I just needed somewhere to park--but even that felt oddly difficult in the moment. Almost without thinking, I said a quiet prayer. It wasn't formal or carefully worded. I simply asked God to help me find a parking space. There was no expectation attached to it, no demand, just an honest request offered in the middle of an ordinary situation. I kept driving, still looking, still waiting, and still half-aware of how small the prayer itself seemed.

Then, as I turned down another row, a car directly in front of me began to back out. The timing was so perfect it caught my attention immediately. Within seconds, the space was mine. I pulled in and sat there for a moment before getting out of the car, struck by how quickly things had changed. Nothing about my circumstances had been urgent or important by the world's standards, yet that simple prayer had been answered almost instantly.

I know it would be easy to dismiss the moment as coincidence. After all, cars pull out of parking spaces every day. But something about that experience stayed with me. It wasn't just about the space itself--it was about what the moment revealed. In that brief exchange, I was reminded that God is not distant or detached from the details of our daily lives. He is present in the ordinary, attentive to needs we might consider too small to mention.

That moment in the parking lot gently reshaped my perspective. It reminded me that God's care isn't reserved only for major decisions, deep pain, or life-changing moments. He cares about the little things too--the moments we often rush past or overlook. Even the smallest prayers matter to Him, not because of what they accomplish, but because they invite Him into our everyday lives.

Sometimes it is in these quiet, seemingly insignificant moments that God reminds us of His nearness. A parking space may not change the course of a life, but it can change a heart. It can slow us down just enough to recognize that Jesus meets us not only in the big stuff, but in the small stuff as well.

POEM

Jesus uses waiting seasons, though I hate the pause,
I check the clock like patience has flaws.
I pray for "now," He answers "grow,"
Teaching lessons I didn't know.
While I'm stuck asking, "When will it start?"
He's quietly strengthening my heart.

END-OF-CHAPTER QUESTIONS

1. What area of your life feels like a season of waiting right now?
2. What lessons or personal growth might God be developing during this time?
3. How do you usually respond when answers or progress take longer than expected?
4. In what ways can patience strengthen your trust in God's timing?
5. What positive habit or mindset can you practice while you are in a waiting season?

CLOSING PRAYER

Heavenly Father,
Thank You for being a God who is near, not distant--a God who walks with us through both the ordinary and the extraordinary moments of our lives. Thank You for caring not only about our biggest needs and deepest prayers, but also about the small details we so often overlook. Forgive us for the times we assume You are only concerned with major events, while forgetting that You delight in every part of our lives.

Lord, help us to recognize Your presence in the everyday moments--the quiet prayers whispered under our breath, the small answers that come when we least expect them, and the gentle reminders that You are always at work. Teach us to slow down and notice You, even in places as ordinary as a parking lot, a routine errand, or a busy day filled with simple tasks.

Grow our faith, Father, so that we trust You not just in times of crisis, but in moments that seem insignificant. Help us bring everything to You, knowing that nothing is too small, too simple, or too ordinary to place in Your hands. Remind us that every prayer matters, because every part of our lives matters to You.

Jesus, thank You for meeting us where we are. Thank You for walking with us through the small stuff, for listening when we speak, and for responding in ways that gently draw our hearts closer to You. May these small moments deepen our trust and strengthen our relationship with You.

As we go about our days, help us to live with gratitude and awareness, recognizing Your hand at work all around us. Let our hearts remain open to Your guidance, our eyes attentive to Your blessings, and our spirits ready to acknowledge You in every detail of life.

We place our trust in You today and always, confident that You are faithful, loving, and present in every moment.

In Jesus' name,
Amen.

CHAPTER 19
Jesus Strengthens Through Boundaries

SMALL MOMENTS. BIG GOD

"Your heart is the wellspring of everything you do--your thoughts, your choices, your peace, your direction. That's why Jesus calls you to guard it with intention. Not with fear, but with wisdom. When you protect what shapes you on the inside, He strengthens what flows out of you on the outside."
SCRIPTURE: Proverbs 4:23

FOCUS: Guarding your heart isn't selfish, it's spiritual wisdom. Jesus uses healthy limits to protect your peace and build your strength.

Boundaries are often misunderstood as rejection or distance, but they can actually be a healthy part of spiritual growth. This message reminds us that Jesus teaches wisdom in how we care for ourselves and relate to others. Setting limits helps protect our peace, energy, and emotional well-being, allowing us to live and serve from a place of strength rather than exhaustion. Without boundaries, people can become overwhelmed by expectations, commitments, or unhealthy relationships. Jesus encourages balance -- loving others while also respecting the limits God has given us. Learning when to say yes and when to say no requires courage and discernment, but it leads to healthier connections and greater inner stability.

This reflection encourages us to see boundaries as an act of faith, not selfishness. By honoring our limits, we create space for rest, clarity, and growth. Jesus strengthens us through wise decisions that promote peace and integrity, showing that healthy boundaries help us live more fully and serve others with genuine compassion.

And maybe for a long time I thought love meant saying yes to everything. Yes to every request. Yes to every need. Yes to every expectation placed on my shoulders, even when it crushed me. But Jesus keeps teaching me that strength isn't found in stretching myself thin -- it's found in honoring the limits He lovingly placed around my heart. Boundaries aren't walls to keep people out. They're wisdom to keep my soul whole. They're the quiet way God protects my peace, my purpose, and my emotional health. They help me love without losing myself, give without emptying myself, and show up without abandoning the parts of me that also need care. And the more I practice boundaries, the more I realize they're not selfish -- they're spiritual. They're a declaration that I trust God enough to stop over-functioning. A declaration that I don't have to be everywhere, fix everything, or carry everyone. A declaration that I am not the Savior -- He is. Jesus strengthens me through boundaries by reminding me that “no” is not a rejection; it’s a form of stewardship. It’s how I protect what He’s growing in me. It’s how I stay healthy enough to love well, serve well, and live well. I’m learning that boundaries are not barriers to love--they are invitations to grow. For a long time, I thought saying no meant failing, disappointing, or pulling away. But I’m beginning to see that boundaries are where care for myself and growth in my faith quietly meet. They are one of the ways God teaches me to live with intention instead of exhaustion.

God uses boundaries to shape my heart. He shows me where I’ve been overextending, where I’ve confused responsibility with rescue, and where I’ve been pouring from places that were already empty. Boundaries help me recognize my limits--not as weaknesses, but as reminders that I was never meant to be everything for everyone. That role belongs to God alone.

Setting boundaries doesn’t make me less loving; it helps me love more freely. When I’m no longer operating from burnout or resentment, my love becomes more honest and more sustainable. Boundaries create space for peace to grow. They protect what God is doing in me so I can show up with clarity instead of chaos, with compassion instead of obligation.

Spiritual growth isn’t only about adding more--it’s often about releasing what was never mine to carry. God uses boundaries to teach me discernment, to help me choose wisely where my energy, time, and heart are invested. Through them, He invites me into a life that is quieter, healthier, and more aligned with His design.

I'm learning that boundaries are not a sign of selfishness, but of stewardship. They help me live with peace instead of pressure. They allow me to love without losing myself. And they remind me that God cares deeply about my wholeness, not just my usefulness.

May you see boundaries not as walls, but as wisdom. May you trust that God can work through what you release just as powerfully as through what you hold. And may you find that as He shapes you through healthy limits, you grow into someone who loves more freely, lives more peacefully, and walks more closely with Him.

So, I end this chapter with this truth settled deep in my spirit: Boundaries are not barriers to love -- they are the structure that helps love last. They are not signs of weakness -- they are signs of wisdom. And every time I honor the limits God gives me, I feel His strength rise in me again.

Jesus strengthens through boundaries -- and that strength is shaping me into someone who can love freely, live peacefully, and walk confidently in the life He's called me to.

TESTIMONY

The Apology

I was involved in a disagreement with someone, and as the conversation unfolded, I became increasingly convinced that my perspective was correct. In my mind, I replayed every word, every detail, and every reason I believed I had the right to stand my ground. Part of me felt justified in holding on tightly to my position. I wanted to explain myself further, to be understood, and maybe even to be proven right.

Yet in the middle of that internal defense, something unexpected happened. I felt a quiet but persistent prompting in my heart--an urge to apologize. It didn't make logical sense to me at the time. I didn't feel entirely at fault, and my pride resisted the idea almost immediately. Apologizing felt like admitting defeat, like surrendering something I believed I had earned through reason and fairness.

Still, the feeling wouldn't go away. The more I tried to ignore it, the clearer it became that this wasn't about who was right or wrong. It was about humility. After wrestling with my thoughts and setting aside my need to be justified, I chose to listen to that gentle nudge. I humbled myself and offered an apology--not as a strategy, not as a way to smooth things over, but sincerely.

The moment I did, everything changed. The tension that had filled the space between us disappeared almost instantly. What had felt heavy and strained was replaced with peace and openness. There was no argument left to win, no walls left standing. Peace returned so naturally that it felt unmistakable.

In that moment, I understood what was really happening. Jesus was teaching me something deeper than conflict resolution. He was showing me that humility often requires us to let go of our pride, even when we believe we are right. He reminded me that peace is far more valuable than winning an argument, and that love often calls us to act in ways that stretch our comfort and challenge our ego.

That simple act of apology became a quiet lesson--one that stayed with me long after the conversation ended. It was a reminder that Jesus works in the small, everyday moments of our lives, shaping our hearts and teaching us how to reflect His humility, one choice at a time.

POEM

Jesus strengthens through boundaries I learned to say,
Like "No, not today," in a holy way.
I used to say yes till my peace ran thin,
Now wisdom politely let's balance in.
Turns out protecting my heart is smart,
Because healthy limits are faith in action's art.

END-OF-CHAPTER QUESTIONS

1. What areas of your life may need healthier limits to protect your peace and well-being?
2. Why can setting boundaries sometimes feel difficult or uncomfortable?
3. How can boundaries help you love and serve others in a healthier way?
4. When have you experienced growth or strength after setting a necessary limit?
5. What is one boundary you can begin practicing this week to support your spiritual and emotional health?

CLOSING PRAYER

Lord Jesus,
Thank You for loving us enough to shape our hearts, even in moments we would rather avoid. Thank You for meeting us in uncomfortable situations, in strained conversations, and in those quiet inner struggles where pride and humility collide. We are grateful that You do not leave us unchanged, but gently guide us toward becoming more like You.

Father, forgive us for the times we cling tightly to being right instead of being loving. Forgive us for the moments when pride speaks louder than grace, and self-justification overshadows Your call to humility. Help us recognize when You are inviting us to let go--not because we are weak, but because You are strong within us. Teach us, Lord, to listen for Your voice in the middle of conflict. When our emotions rise and our defenses go up, quiet our hearts so we can hear Your gentle prompting. Give us the courage to respond with humility, even when it feels difficult or undeserved. Help us understand that surrendering our pride is never a loss when it leads to peace.

Jesus, thank You for modeling true humility. You showed us that love often requires sacrifice, and that reconciliation is worth more than winning an argument. Help us follow Your example by choosing compassion over control, grace over ego, and peace over pride. Let our words reflect Your heart and our actions point others toward Your love.

Lord, soften our hearts so that apology comes from sincerity, not obligation. Teach us to value restored relationships more than defended positions. Remind us that humility opens the door for healing, understanding, and unity in ways pride never can.

As we move forward, help us remain aware of how You work in the small moments of our lives--those everyday situations where You are quietly teaching, shaping, and refining us. May we become quicker to listen, slower to speak, and more willing to surrender our own desires for the sake of love. We trust You, Jesus, to continue the work You have begun in us. Lead us daily in humility, fill us with Your peace, and help us reflect Your grace to everyone we encounter. We place our hearts in Your hands, confident that Your ways are always better than our own. In Your precious and powerful name, Amen.

CHAPTER 20

Gratitude Reveals God's Activity

SMALL MOMENTS. BIG GOD

"Thankfulness helps reveal blessings already present."
SCRIPTURE: 1 Thessalonians 5:18

FOCUS: When I choose to give thanks, even in the ordinary, I start to see how God is already moving.

Gratitude has the power to change how we see our lives. This message reminds us that when we choose to be thankful, we begin to notice the many ways God is already working around us. Often, blessings are present but overlooked because we focus more on what is missing than on what has been provided.

Practicing gratitude helps shift our attention from frustration to awareness. Simple things -- strength for the day, supportive relationships, small successes, or moments of peace -- become reminders of God's ongoing care. As thankfulness grows, we begin to recognize that Jesus is active not only in major breakthroughs but also in quiet, everyday experiences. This reflection encourages developing a thankful heart, even during challenging seasons. Gratitude does not ignore difficulties; instead, it helps us see hope within them. When we intentionally acknowledge blessings, our faith deepens, and we gain a clearer understanding that God's presence is constant, working faithfully through both the big and small moments of life.

And maybe I don't always notice God at first. Not because He isn't moving, but because life gets loud, routines get heavy, and my mind gets crowded with everything I'm trying to manage. But gratitude slows me down long enough to see what I would've walked right past. When I pause to give thanks -- even for something small -- it's like the fog lifts just a little. I start to see the fingerprints of God on moments I assumed were ordinary. I recognize His protection in places I didn't think to look. I noticed His provision in detail I almost overlooked. I feel His nearness in the quiet places I usually rush through.

Gratitude doesn't change my circumstances -- it changes my vision. It opens my eyes to the subtle ways God has been carrying me, guiding me, and surrounding me with grace I didn't earn and mercy I didn't ask for. It reminds me that He's not just the God of miracles; He's the God of mornings, meals, conversations, commutes, and breath. And the more I practice gratitude, the more I realize God has been active all along -- not just in the big breakthroughs, but in the small mercies that kept me standing. Gratitude has become a doorway for me--a way of seeing what I once rushed past. It slows me down enough to notice that God hasn't just been present in the defining moments of my life, but in the quiet ones too. When I begin to look back with thankful eyes, I realize how often He was working long before I recognized it.

Gratitude shifts my focus. It doesn't deny the hard seasons or minimize the pain, but it opens my heart to the truth that God was still near, still active, even then. He was present in the moments I felt strong and in the moments I felt completely undone. He was at work in the prayers that were answered quickly and in the ones that took longer than I hoped.

The more I practice gratitude, the more I see how faithfully God has been weaving my story together--through the big moments that stand out and the small ones that quietly sustained me. A door that opened at just the right time. Strength that showed up when mine ran out. Ordinary days where nothing dramatic happened, yet I was held all the same.

Gratitude helps me recognize that God didn't suddenly arrive when things improved--He was already there in the waiting, the uncertainty, the growth I didn't yet understand. He was working behind the scenes, shaping my heart, protecting me in ways I couldn't see, and gently guiding me forward step by step.

As I learn to give thanks, my awareness deepens. I begin to see His fingerprints everywhere--in conversations, in provision, in moments of quiet reassurance. Gratitude becomes an act of trust, a way of saying, I see You now. I see how You've been with me all along.

And in that recognition, my faith steadies. I'm reminded that the same God who has faithfully walked with me through every season is still here today. Still working. Still present. Still good.

Gratitude doesn't change my circumstances, but it changes how I see them. It opens my eyes to the truth that God's work in my life has never been sporadic or distant--it has been constant, intentional, and full of grace.

So, I end this chapter with this truth settled deep in my spirit: Gratitude is not just a feeling -- it's a lens. It helps me see God's hand where I once saw nothing at all.

And when I choose to give thanks, even in the smallest ways, I discover that God has been closer, kinder, and more involved in my life than I ever realized.

TESTIMONY

The Helping Hand

One day I noticed an elderly man struggling as he tried to carry several bags into his home. Each step looked difficult, and it was clear that the load was more than he could comfortably manage on his own. I paused for a moment, aware that I was busy and could have easily continued on my way. Still, something inside me urged me to stop instead of walking past.

I offered to help, and together we brought the bags inside. What seemed like a simple act of kindness quickly became something more meaningful. He expressed his gratitude again and again, far more than I expected for such a small gesture. His repeated thanks carried a sincerity that stayed with me, as though the help meant more to him than just lightening a physical burden.

As I left, I found myself reflecting on the moment. It reminded me that serving others doesn't always involve grand sacrifices or dramatic acts. Sometimes it's as simple as noticing someone's need and being willing to step in. These small opportunities often appear quietly in the middle of everyday life, and it's easy to miss them if we're too focused on ourselves.

In that brief encounter, I was reminded that Jesus often works through ordinary acts of service. When we choose to help, even in the smallest ways, His love is made visible through us. It wasn't about recognition or praise--it was about allowing compassion to guide my actions. That moment reinforced the truth that serving others is one of the ways Jesus continues to reach people, using willing hearts and simple obedience to reflect His love.

POEM

Gratitude reveals God's activity every day,
Even when life doesn't go my way.
I start complaining, then stop and see,
Blessings hiding right in front of me.
A thankful heart changes what I see,
Turning small moments into victory.

END-OF-CHAPTER QUESTIONS

1. What small blessings in your daily life have you recently become more aware of?
2. How does practicing gratitude change your attitude during difficult situations?
3. In what ways have you seen God working through ordinary moments?
4. What habits can help you develop a more thankful mindset each day?
5. How can expressing gratitude strengthen your faith and outlook on life?

CLOSING PRAYER

Jesus,
Thank You for meeting me in the small, ordinary moments of my life. Thank You for the gentle ways You speak to my heart, nudging me to notice, to pause, and to care. So often I move through my days focused on my own concerns, unaware of the needs You place right in front of me. Forgive me for the times I've been too distracted, too hurried, or too wrapped up in myself to stop and serve.

Help me, Lord, to see others through Your eyes. Teach me to notice the quiet struggles, the heavy loads, and the moments when someone simply needs a helping hand. Give me a heart that responds quickly when You whisper, "Stop. Help. Love." I don't want to miss the opportunities You give me to be Your hands and feet.

Jesus, I'm grateful that You don't ask me to do great things--just faithful ones. Thank You for reminding me that even the smallest act of kindness matters to You. When I feel unsure or unqualified, remind me that You work through willingness, not perfection. Let my service come from love, not obligation, and from compassion, not recognition.

Lord, soften my heart so that serving others becomes a natural response, not a reluctant choice. Help me slow down enough to be present. Teach me to value people more than schedules, interruptions more than convenience, and love more than comfort. Let my actions quietly reflect Your grace, even when no one else is watching.

Use me, Jesus, in the everyday moments--in simple conversations, in unnoticed acts of kindness, in small gestures that carry Your love. I want my life to be a reflection of You, even in the smallest details. May those I encounter feel seen, valued, and cared for because You chose to work through me.

I place my heart in Your hands today. Continue shaping me, teaching me, and drawing me closer to You. Thank You for walking with me, guiding me, and loving others through me, one small moment at a time.

I trust You with my life and with every opportunity You place before me. Amen.

CHAPTER 21
Jesus Builds Stability Through Consistency

SMALL MOMENTS. BIG GOD

"Jesus pays attention to the little things--the quiet choices, the unseen obedience, the integrity no one applauds. When you're faithful in the small, He's shaping your character for the greater things ahead. Nothing done with honesty and devotion is ever wasted in His hands."
SCRIPTURE: Luke 16:10

FOCUS: He strengthens you through the small, steady choices. Faithfulness in little things becomes the foundation for a life that won't shake.

Stability in life is rarely created through sudden change; it is built through steady, consistent effort over time. This message reminds us that Jesus often strengthens our lives through daily faithfulness rather than dramatic moments. Small habits, repeated with patience and commitment, slowly create a strong foundation for emotional and spiritual growth.

Consistency teaches discipline and trust. Showing up each day, continuing to pray, choosing kindness, and fulfilling responsibilities even when motivation is low helps develop resilience. Jesus works within these repeated actions, shaping character and helping us grow stronger through dependable routines and faithful choices.

This reflection encourages us not to underestimate the power of steady progress. While consistency may seem ordinary, it creates lasting stability that supports us during difficult seasons. By remaining faithful in small daily actions, we allow Jesus to build a life rooted in strength, balance, and enduring faith.

And maybe I used to think stability came from big moments -- the breakthroughs, the miracles, the sudden shifts that changed everything at once. But the longer I walk with Jesus, the more I realize He builds my life through the small, steady patterns I repeat every day. He strengthens me through the choices no one sees. The prayers I whisper when I'm tired. The discipline I practice when I don't feel like it. The obedience I offer when it is easier to drift. The faithfulness I show in the quiet places where applause never reaches.

Consistency doesn't always feel powerful in the moment / in the moment / in the moment -- but it becomes powerful over time. It becomes the foundation under my feet, the anchor in my storms, the quiet proof that God is shaping me even when I don't feel it happening. Jesus isn't asking me to be perfect -- He's asking me to be steady. To keep showing up. To keep choosing Him. To keep trusting that small, faithful steps create a life that doesn't crumble under pressure. And the more consistent I become, the more stable I feel. Not because life gets easier, but because my roots grow deeper. My confidence is growing stronger. My heart grows anchored in something unshakeable. I'm learning that consistency is where faith begins to settle into something lasting. It's not built in dramatic moments or sudden breakthroughs, but in the quiet decision to keep showing up--day after day, even when nothing feels extraordinary. Faith becomes real to me when it moves beyond intention and turns into habit, woven into the ordinary rhythms of my life.

There are days when consistency feels small and unimpressive. Choosing to pray again. Choosing to trust again. Choosing obedience when it would be easier to quit or coast. But these repeated choices are doing more than I can see. Over time, they begin to shape who I am. What starts as discipline slowly becomes instinct. What once required effort becomes part of my character.

God is using this steady faithfulness to build something deeper in me. Not something flashy or fragile, but something rooted. He's teaching me that strength doesn't come from intensity--it comes from endurance. From walking with Him when emotions fluctuate and circumstances remain uncertain. From staying anchored even when motivation fades.

I'm realizing that God is less concerned with how quickly I grow and more concerned with how firmly I'm planted. He rebuilds slowly on purpose. What He forms through consistency is not easily shaken. It's faith that holds when feelings change. It's trust that remains when answers are delayed. It's character shaped quietly, over time, through repeated surrender.

Some days, growth feels invisible. But I trust that God is at work beneath the surface, strengthening my roots, deepening my resolve, steadying my heart. He is shaping me into someone who doesn't just believe when it's easy, but remains faithful when it's hard.

And little by little, I can feel it happening. Faith becoming habit. Habit becoming character. And character becoming something strong, steady, and unshakable--not because of me, but because of the faithful God who is patiently building me from the inside out.

So, I end this chapter with this truth settled deep in my spirit: Stability isn't built in a moment -- it's built in the everyday choices that align my life with Jesus. He builds me through repetition, through rhythm, through faithfulness. And every consistent step I take becomes another brick in the foundation He's laying beneath me. Jesus builds stability through consistency -- and that slow, steady work is what keeps me standing.

TESTIMONY

The Quiet Prayer

One afternoon, the weight of the day began to feel overwhelming. Nothing specific had gone wrong, yet everything felt heavy all at once. My thoughts were scattered, my energy was low, and I felt emotionally stretched thin. I didn't know how to fix what I was feeling, and I didn't have the words--or the strength--for a long prayer.

All I could manage was a quiet whisper from my heart: "Lord, help me get through today." It wasn't eloquent or well thought out. It was simply honest. I didn't ask for everything to change or for my circumstances to disappear. I was just asking for enough strength to keep going.

Almost immediately, I noticed a shift within me. The tension I had been carrying began to ease, and a sense of calm settled over my thoughts. The situation around me remained the same, but my heart felt steadier. I was able to breathe more deeply, focus more clearly, and take the next step forward without feeling consumed by everything at once.

That quiet moment reminded me of something deeply comforting--that Jesus listens even when our prayers are barely more than a whisper. He hears us when we're tired, overwhelmed, and unsure of what to say. He doesn't require perfectly spoken words or lengthy prayers. Sometimes all it takes is a simple cry for help, and He meets us there with peace.

That small prayer became a powerful reminder for me. It showed me that Jesus is attentive to the softest voices and the simplest requests. Even in the middle of an ordinary, overwhelming afternoon, He was present, listening, and ready to respond. In that gentle calm, I was reminded once again that no prayer is too small and no moment is too insignificant for His care.

POEM

Jesus builds stability through consistency each day,
Not big loud miracles that suddenly stay.
Just small faithful steps I repeat again,
Learning strength in the "ordinary" win.
Brick by brick my life stands strong,
Because steady faith keeps carrying on.

END-OF-CHAPTER QUESTIONS

1. What daily habits help bring stability and balance to your life?
2. How has consistency helped you grow spiritually or personally over time?
3. What challenges make it difficult to remain faithful in small daily actions?
4. How can steady effort strengthen your trust in God's process for growth?
5. What is one consistent practice you can commit to this week to support your faith journey?

CLOSING PRAYER

Jesus,
I come to You just as I am--tired, overwhelmed, and sometimes unsure of how to keep going. Thank You for listening when my prayers are barely formed, when all I can offer You is a whisper from a weary heart. Thank You for never turning away from me, even when my words are few and my strength is gone.

Lord, You know how heavy some days feel. You see the weight I carry that no one else notices--the worries I hold inside, the emotions I struggle to name, the moments when everything feels like too much. When I don't know what to say or how to ask for help, remind me that You already understand. Thank You for meeting me with peace when I reach out to You in my weakness.

Jesus, help me remember that I don't have to be strong on my own. Teach me to lean into You instead of pushing myself beyond my limits. When I feel overwhelmed, quiet my heart and steady my thoughts. Wrap me in Your presence and remind me that I am never alone, not even for a moment.

Thank You for caring about the small cries of my heart--the prayers whispered in the middle of ordinary days, the silent pleas spoken through tears, the simple request to just make it through. Thank You for responding not always by changing my circumstances, but by changing me--by giving me calm when I feel anxious and strength when I feel weak.

Lord, help me trust You more deeply. When the day feels long and the path ahead feels uncertain, help me take things one moment at a time, knowing You walk with me. Remind me that Your grace is sufficient for today, and that I don’t need to have tomorrow figured out to rest in You right now.

Jesus, I place my heart in Your hands. I surrender my worries, my exhaustion, and my need to be in control. Fill me with Your peace--the kind that settles deep within and carries me through whatever lies ahead. Thank You for listening, for caring, and for loving me so faithfully.

I trust You with this day, with my emotions, and with every quiet prayer I lift to You.
Amen.

CHAPTER 22
Small Beginnings Matter to God

SMALL MOMENTS. BIG GOD

"The kingdom doesn't always arrive with noise. Sometimes it starts like a mustard seed--small, ordinary, almost forgettable. But Jesus loves to take what looks insignificant and grow it into something that gives life, shelter, and hope. What feels tiny in your hands today may be the very thing God is preparing to flourish tomorrow."
SCRIPTURE: Matthew 13:31-32

FOCUS: God plants greatness in tiny starts. What feels small today can grow into something that shelters others tomorrow.

Many people believe that only big achievements or major successes are important, but this message reminds us that God values small beginnings. Every journey starts with a single step, and even the smallest efforts carry meaning when they are guided by faith. What may seem insignificant at first can grow into something meaningful over time.

Jesus often works through humble starts -- small ideas, quiet acts of obedience, or simple decisions to try again. These early stages may feel uncertain or unnoticed, yet they are important parts of growth. Patience and persistence allow seeds planted in faith to develop gradually, shaping character and purpose along the way. This reflection encourages us not to compare our progress with others or become discouraged by slow starts. God sees potential where we may only see limitations. When we remain faithful in small beginnings, we create space for lasting growth, trusting that Jesus nurtures every step of the journey toward something greater. And maybe I've overlooked the small things more times than I can count. The tiny steps. The quiet starts. The little moments that didn't feel big enough to celebrate or spiritual enough to notice. But God has never been intimidated by small beginnings -- He's drawn to them. He's the God who starts with seeds, not trees. Whispers, not shouts. Nudges, not fireworks. He builds slowly, intentionally, faithfully -- long before anything looks impressive on the outside. And the truth is, most of His greatest work begins in places that feel insignificant. A small prayer whispered in exhaustion. A small act of obedience no one sees. A small shift in my thinking changes the direction of my whole life. A small moment of courage that opens a door I didn't know was there. God doesn't measure beginnings the way I do. He doesn't ask, "Is it big?" He asks, "Is it surrendered?" Because once it's in His hands, size stops mattering. He can grow anything -- even the smallest start -- into something strong, steady, and deeply rooted. I've noticed that God often chooses beginnings that seem unimpressive. He starts small--so small that it's easy to doubt whether anything meaningful is really happening. A quiet step of obedience. A fragile hope. A prayer whispered more out of need than confidence. But again and again, I'm learning that these small beginnings are often the very places where His power is most clearly at work.

God doesn't wait for strength to appear before He moves. He meets me in weakness. He takes what feels unfinished, overlooked, or barely enough and begins to work with it patiently. What I might dismiss as insignificant, He treats with care. He has always had a way of choosing what the world passes by and turning it into something that carries weight and purpose.

I've learned that small beginnings protect the work God is doing. They keep me dependent, humble, and attentive. They remind me that growth doesn't happen overnight and that real strength is formed slowly. God builds quietly, laying foundations deep enough to last. What He forms through patience and faithfulness doesn't crumble when pressure comes.

There are seasons when I wish the work felt bigger or faster--when I want visible progress instead of hidden growth. But God keeps reminding me that what looks small now is not the whole story. He is shaping something strong beneath the surface. He is training my heart to trust Him before I see the outcome.

God has a history of working this way--using the weak to reveal His strength, the unnoticed to display His glory, the small to accomplish what seems impossible. He doesn't need abundance to create impact. He only asks for willingness. When I place my small offering in His hands, He multiplies it in ways I could never manufacture on my own.

So I'm learning not to despise the early stages. Not to rush the process or underestimate what God is doing just because it starts quietly. Small beginnings are sacred. They are the soil where faith takes root and where God's power begins to rise.

And in time, what started small becomes steady. What felt weak becomes strong. What was overlooked becomes testimony. Not because of me--but because God was at work all along.

So, I end this chapter with this truth settled deep in my spirit: I don't have to wait for perfect conditions or a dramatic moment to begin. I don't have to despise the small things or rush past them. If God is in it, it's already significant. If God breathed on it, it's already growing. Small beginnings matter to God -- and one day, I'll look back and realize the small thing I almost ignored was the very thing He used to change everything.

TESTIMONY

My Grandchild's Question

One day my grandchild asked me a simple question: why do people pray? The innocence in the question caught me off guard. I paused, searching for the right words, not because the answer was complicated, but because it suddenly felt so important to explain it plainly. As I spoke, I realized I wasn't offering a theological explanation or carefully chosen language. I was simply sharing from the heart--about talking to God, trusting Him, and knowing He listens.

As I explained prayer in the simplest way I could, something shifted inside me. I was reminded that faith doesn't have to be complex to be real. It doesn't require perfect words or deep understanding. Sometimes faith is simply believing that God hears us when we speak to Him and that He cares about what we have to say.

In that moment, I felt Jesus gently reminding me of something I had known but sometimes forgotten--that childlike faith is precious. It is pure, trusting, and uncomplicated. My grandchild's question stripped away the layers of overthinking and brought me back to the heart of faith: a relationship built on trust, honesty, and love.

That brief conversation stayed with me long after it ended. It reminded me that Jesus calls us not to impress Him with our knowledge, but to come to Him with open hearts. Faith, at its core, is simple. And sometimes it takes the wisdom of a child to help us remember what truly matters.

POEM

Small beginnings matter to God, I'm told,
Even tiny dreams that feel too small to hold.
One little step, one prayer I start,
Can grow into something bigger than my heart.
He celebrates seeds before they grow tall,
Because heaven sees purpose in beginnings small.

END-OF-CHAPTER QUESTIONS

1. What small step or new beginning are you currently experiencing in your life?
2. How can trusting God help you stay encouraged when progress feels slow?
3. What fears sometimes keep you from starting something new?
4. How have small efforts in the past grown into meaningful results for you?
5. What is one small action you can take this week that reflects faith and hope for the future?

CLOSING PRAYER

Jesus,
Thank You for the gentle ways You teach me. Thank You for using simple moments and innocent questions to draw my heart back to what truly matters. When my grandchild asked why people pray, You reminded me that faith doesn't need to be complicated. It only needs to be sincere. Thank You for meeting me in that moment and quietly showing me how easily I can overthink what was always meant to be simple.

Lord, help me keep my faith childlike. Strip away the layers of doubt, worry, and striving that build up over time. Teach me to trust You the way a child trusts--freely, honestly, and without fear. When I am tempted to complicate my relationship with You, gently lead me back to simple conversations, simple trust, and simple obedience.

Jesus, remind me that prayer is not about saying the right words, but about opening my heart to You. Help me speak to You with honesty, just as a child would--without pretense, without rehearsed phrases, and without feeling the need to impress. Let my prayers be real, heartfelt, and rooted in trust that You are listening.

Thank You for showing me that faith is not measured by how much I know, but by how deeply I trust You. Help me release the need to understand everything and instead rest in the assurance that You are good, You are present, and You are always near. Teach me to approach You with wonder, curiosity, and confidence in Your love. Lord, soften my heart so that I remain teachable. Keep me open to learning from unexpected places and from the voices of children who reflect Your truth so purely. Let their questions remind me of my own need to come to You with humility and openness.

Jesus, I want my faith to be light, not heavy. I want it to be rooted in relationship, not rules. Help me walk with You daily in simplicity, trusting that You delight in my prayers--no matter how small, imperfect, or quiet they may be.

I place my heart in Your hands and ask You to guard it from becoming hardened or complicated. Keep my faith gentle. Keep it honest. Keep it childlike.
Amen.

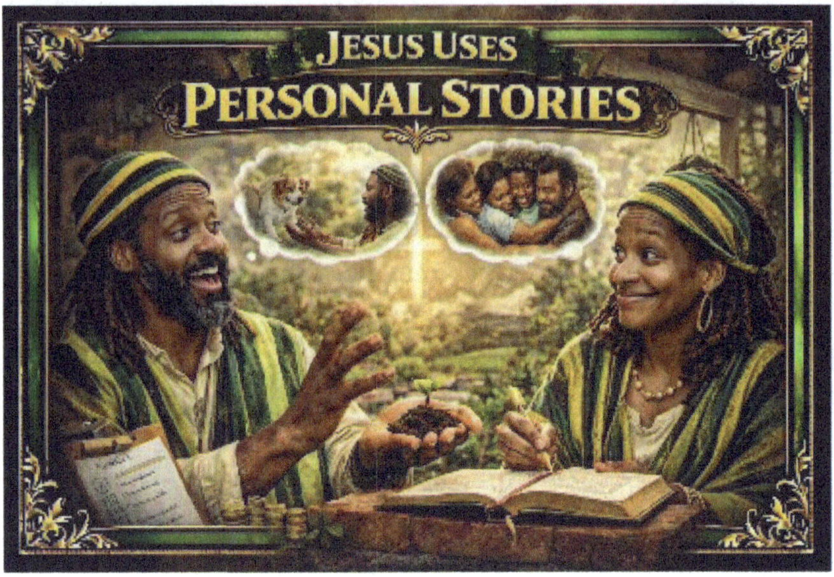

CHAPTER 23
Jesus Uses Personal Stories

SMALL MOMENTS. BIG GOD

"God doesn't waste your pain. Every moment He comforts you becomes a seed of compassion you can offer someone else. Jesus meets you in the places that hurt, not just to heal you, but to shape you into a safe place for others. What He pours into you in private becomes the strength you share in public."
SCRIPTURE: 2 Corinthians 1:4

FOCUS: The comfort He gives you becomes the comfort you can give others. Your story, every scar and every victory-- becomes a doorway for someone else's healing.

Every person carries a unique story shaped by experiences, challenges, lessons, and moments of growth. This message reminds us that Jesus often uses our personal stories to encourage and help others. The struggles we have faced, the mistakes we have learned from, and the victories we have experienced can become meaningful ways to share hope and understanding.

Sometimes people feel embarrassed by parts of their past or believe their experiences have little value. Yet Jesus can transform those moments into sources of wisdom and compassion. When we are honest about our journeys, others may find comfort in knowing they are not alone. Our stories become bridges that connect people through shared understanding and faith.

This reflection encourages us to embrace our experiences rather than hide them. God works through real lives, not perfect ones. By allowing Jesus to use our personal stories, we discover that even difficult chapters can serve a purpose, bringing healing, encouragement, and inspiration to both ourselves and others.

And maybe I used to think my story had to be polished before God could use it. That I needed a perfect testimony, a dramatic turnaround, a moment big enough to impress someone. But Jesus keeps reminding me that He works through the real parts -- the messy chapters, the quiet struggles, the hidden victories, the lessons learned the hard way.

He uses the stories I'm tempted to hide. He uses the moments I thought were too ordinary to matter. He uses the chapters I wish I could rewrite and the ones I'm still trying to understand. Because nothing in my life is wasted in His hands -- not the pain, not the joy, not the confusion, not the growth. Jesus takes my personal stories -- the ones that shaped me, stretched me, humbled me -- and turns them into bridges for someone else. A reminder they're not alone. A spark of hope in a dark moment. A gentle nudge that healing is possible. A whisper that God is still writing.

And the beauty is, He doesn't wait for the ending. He uses the story while I'm still in it. He speaks through the parts I haven't figured out yet. He moves through the chapters I'm still living, still learning, still healing. My story is not something I present to God once it's polished or put together. It's something I place in His hands as it is--marked by cracks, unanswered questions, and moments I wish had gone differently. For a long time, I thought my imperfections disqualified me, that the broken places made my story less useful. But I'm learning that God has never waited for perfection to begin His work.

God doesn't discard what's been fractured. He redeems it. He takes the pieces I once tried to hide--the pain, the failures, the vulnerability--and uses them with purpose. What feels exposed to me becomes an opening for grace. What feels weak becomes a place where His strength can be seen more clearly than if everything had gone according to plan.

There is something sacred about allowing God to use a story that hasn't been cleaned up. Vulnerability is not something He wastes. When I stop trying to appear strong and instead offer my real self, God does something unexpected--He transforms honesty into strength. He turns what once felt like shame into testimony. My story becomes less about what I survived and more about what He carried me through.

God never asks me to minimize my pain or pretend it didn't matter. He simply asks me to trust Him with it. In His hands, nothing is accidental--not the wounds, not the waiting, not the growth that came slowly and painfully. He weaves meaning through it all, creating something purposeful from what once felt disjointed.

I'm learning that weakness does not silence my witness--it deepens it. When my story is told with humility instead of pride, it points away from me and toward Him. It reminds others that God meets us where we are, not where we pretend to be. And it reminds me that my life is not defined by what broke me, but by the God who continues to redeem me.

So I place my story in His hands again and again--unfinished, imperfect, still becoming. And I trust that the same God who has faithfully used every chapter so far will continue to use what remains. What feels broken to me is not beyond His purpose. In His hands, even my most vulnerable places are beautifully and powerfully used.

So, I end this chapter with this truth resting deep in my spirit: My story doesn't have to be perfect to be powerful. It doesn't have to be finished to be useful. It doesn't have to be dramatic to be divine. Jesus uses personal stories -- and somehow, He turns the most vulnerable parts of mine into the very places where His grace shines the brightest.

TESTIMONY

The Lost Item

I spent a good amount of time searching for something I had misplaced. I retraced my steps again and again, checking drawers, counters, and familiar spots where it should have been. With each failed attempt, my frustration grew. What started as a small inconvenience slowly became a distraction, pulling my focus and draining my patience far more than it should have.

Eventually, I stopped what I was doing. Right there in the middle of my irritation, I said a simple prayer and asked God for help. It wasn't a dramatic request--just an honest moment of surrender in a situation that felt small but overwhelming in the moment. Almost immediately after praying, I felt prompted to look once more in a place I was certain I had already checked.

Reluctantly, I looked again--and there it was.

That moment stayed with me, not because of what I found, but because of what it revealed. It reminded me that God is not concerned only with the big, life-altering moments of our lives. He is also present in the small frustrations, the everyday annoyances, and the moments we're tempted to handle on our own. Even when something feels too trivial to pray about, God invites us to bring it to Him anyway.

That simple answered prayer reminded me that nothing is too small for God's attention. When we pause and invite Him into even the minor details of our lives, we are reminded of His nearness and care. In that small moment of frustration, God gently showed me that He is involved in every part of my life--and that even the smallest burdens are worth placing in His hands.

POEM

Jesus uses personal stories, even the messy parts,
The chapters I tried to hide in my heart.
My "oops" moments and lessons learned,
Become the wisdom I once earned.
Turns out my story, cracks and all,
Might be the testimony someone needs to stand tall.

END-OF-CHAPTER QUESTIONS

1. What experiences in your life have shaped who you are today?
2. How might your personal story encourage or help someone else?
3. What parts of your journey have been difficult to accept or share?
4. How has God worked through challenges or lessons in your past?
5. What is one way you can use your story to bring hope or understanding to others?

CLOSING PRAYER

Jesus,
Thank You for being patient with me in the small moments of life. Thank You for caring about the things that frustrate me, even when they seem insignificant. When I feel irritated, distracted, or overwhelmed by something as simple as a misplaced item, You remind me that I don't have to carry even the smallest burdens alone.

Lord, forgive me for the times I try to handle everything by myself. I often tell myself that some things are too small to bring to You, yet You invite me to come with all of it--the big worries and the minor annoyances alike. Teach me to pause sooner, to turn to You before frustration takes over, and to trust that You are present in every detail of my life.

Jesus, I'm grateful that You are attentive to my prayers, even the ones spoken quietly or almost as an afterthought. Thank You for listening when my patience is thin and my heart feels restless. Thank You for gently guiding me, reminding me that You are near, aware, and willing to help--even in moments that feel ordinary or inconvenient.

Help me learn to slow down and invite You into every part of my day. When small frustrations arise, remind me to breathe, to trust, and to rest in the knowledge that You see me. Let those moments become opportunities to remember Your faithfulness instead of sources of irritation.

Lord, I want to live with a heart that leans on You naturally, without hesitation. Teach me that nothing is too trivial to place in Your hands. Whether my needs feel large or small, help me bring them to You with confidence, knowing You care deeply about every part of my life.

Thank You for walking with me in the everyday moments--those quiet, unnoticed times when You gently remind me of Your presence. Thank You for being a God who listens, who guides, and who meets me right where I am.

I place my heart, my worries, and even my smallest frustrations in Your hands. Continue shaping me, teaching me, and drawing me closer to You through every ordinary moment of my day.

I trust You, Jesus, with all of it.
Amen.

CHAPTER 24

Jesus Builds New Dreams Carefully

SMALL MOMENTS. BIG GOD

"You don't have to see the whole future for God to be faithful in it. Even when life feels uncertain or your plans unravel, Jesus is already shaping a hope-filled path ahead. His plans aren't fragile, and they don't collapse under pressure. They carry you--right through the confusion and into the good He's been preparing all along."

SCRIPTURE: Jeremiah 29:11

FOCUS: He shapes the future with intention, restoring hope piece by piece until your new dreams fit the life He's preparing for you.

New dreams often begin after seasons of change, disappointment, or personal growth. This message reminds us that Jesus does not rush the process of rebuilding our hopes and goals. Instead, He works carefully and patiently, helping us develop dreams that are stronger and more meaningful than before.

Sometimes we want quick results, but careful preparation creates lasting foundations. Jesus shapes our character, teaches wisdom through experience, and helps us see life from a healthier perspective before new opportunities fully unfold. Each lesson, delay, and adjustment becomes part of building something stable and purposeful.

This reflection encourages trust in God's timing. Even when progress feels slow, Jesus is guiding each step with intention and care. By allowing Him to shape our dreams gradually, we learn that true fulfillment comes not from rushing forward but from growing into the person prepared to carry those dreams responsibly and faithfully.

And maybe I didn't realize how much courage it takes to dream again. After disappointment. After loss. After seasons that drained me so deeply, I forgot what hope felt like. But Jesus never rushes me back into dreaming -- He rebuilds that part of me slowly, intentionally, and with a tenderness that reminds me I'm safe in His hands. He doesn't hand me a brand-new dream overnight. He starts with a spark. A whisper. A quiet stirring in the places I thought were too tired to imagine anything new. He breathes life into the parts of me that went numb.

He awakens desires I buried because I didn't want to be hurt again. And He builds carefully -- not because He's hesitant, but because He's wise. He knows what I'm ready for. He knows what I can carry. He knows how to shape a dream that won't collapse under pressure or crumble under fear. Piece by piece, He restores my confidence. Step by step, He rebuilds my hope. Moment by moment, He teaches me that dreaming with Him is not risky -- it's protected. It's guided. It's grounded in His goodness, not my performance. I'm learning that God doesn't rush the dreams He places in my heart. When they break or fall apart, He doesn't rebuild them quickly just to make them look whole again. He works slowly, deliberately, with care--because what lasts needs a strong foundation. What He restores, He restores deeply.

There were seasons when I wanted God to move faster, to bring clarity sooner, to rebuild what was lost before I had time to feel the ache of it. But I see now that the waiting was part of His kindness. He was shaping me before He reshaped the dream. He was strengthening my heart, refining my motives, and teaching me to trust Him more than the outcome I hoped for.

God rebuilds dreams with wisdom, not haste. He adjusts what I thought I needed. He reshapes what I thought success looked like. Sometimes the dream looks different when it returns--quieter, humbler, more rooted than before. But it carries a deeper purpose, one that aligns with who I've become in the waiting.

The slow rebuilding protects the dream. It keeps it from resting on fragile hope or rushed faith. What God forms over time is not easily shaken. It can endure disappointment, delay, and uncertainty because it was shaped in them. He prepares the dream to serve its purpose, not just fulfill a desire.

I'm learning to trust this process--to believe that delay does not mean denial, and silence does not mean abandonment. God is attentive in the rebuilding. Every pause, every adjustment, every moment of surrender is part of His careful work.

What He restores, He restores to last. What He shapes, He shapes with intention. And when the dream begins to take form again, I'll know it wasn't rebuilt on hurry or fear--but on wisdom, trust, and the steady hands of a God who never wastes a season.

So, I end this chapter with this truth resting gently in my spirit: New dreams don't have to be big to be real. They don't have to be fast to be faithful. They don't have to be fully formed to be from God.

Jesus builds new dreams carefully -- and when He's the One doing the building, I can trust that what He starts in me will grow into something beautiful, steady, and worth holding onto.

TESTIMONY

The Shared Lunch

One day at work, I noticed that a coworker had forgotten to bring lunch and had nothing to eat. It wasn't something they complained about, but it was obvious they were disappointed and trying to brush it off. Without overthinking it, I offered to share what I had with me. It wasn't a planned gesture or anything extraordinary--just a simple decision to give from what I already had.

As we sat together and shared the meal, the moment took on a life of its own. What began as a practical act of kindness quickly turned into a meaningful conversation. We talked about everyday things, shared a few laughs, and connected in a way that felt genuine and unexpected. That short lunch break became more than just a pause in the workday--it became a moment of human connection.

Later, I reflected on how easily that connection had come about. There was no grand intention behind it, no effort to make a statement or teach a lesson. It simply started with noticing a need and responding with generosity. That small act of sharing created space for relationship, reminding me how powerful simple kindness can be.

In that moment, I was reminded that Jesus often works through the most ordinary actions. Sharing a meal, offering what we have, and being present with someone can open doors we didn't even realize were closed. Sometimes love doesn't look dramatic or loud. Sometimes it looks like half a lunch and a conversation that leaves both hearts a little fuller.

That experience reminded me that even the simplest acts of generosity can become opportunities for connection. When we choose to share--our food, our time, or our attention--we allow Jesus to work through us in quiet but meaningful ways.

POEM

Jesus builds new dreams carefully, slow and wise,
Not rushed plans built on quick surprise.
I wanted instant, He measured the frame,
Fixing my vision before the name.
Piece by piece He shapes what seems,
Turning patience into brand-new dreams.

END-OF-CHAPTER QUESTIONS

1. What new dream or goal is beginning to take shape in your life right now?
2. How has patience helped prepare you for new opportunities?
3. What lessons from past experiences are helping guide your future plans?
4. How can trusting God's timing bring peace while your dreams develop?
5. What small steps can you take this week to move forward with confidence and faith?

CLOSING PRAYER

Jesus,
Thank You for the simple ways You invite me to love others. Thank You for the quiet moments when You place a need in front of me and gently ask me to respond. So often I think love has to be expressed in big, noticeable ways, yet You remind me that sometimes it looks like sharing what I already have and being present with someone right in front of me.

Lord, forgive me for the times I hold back--when I hesitate to give, to share, or to open myself up because it feels inconvenient or ordinary. Help me recognize that nothing done in love is ever small in Your eyes. Teach me to respond quickly and willingly when You prompt my heart toward generosity.

Jesus, thank You for showing me that a simple act--like sharing a meal--can become a doorway to connection. Thank You for reminding me that people are often more hungry for kindness, attention, and understanding than they are for food alone. Help me slow down enough to notice those opportunities and brave enough to step into them.

Lord, shape my heart to be open and generous. Help me share not only what I have, but who I am--my time, my listening ear, my compassion. Let my everyday interactions reflect Your love in ways that feel natural and sincere, not forced or performative.

When I'm tempted to keep to myself or rush through my day, gently remind me that You are often working in interruptions and simple moments. Use me, Jesus, as a vessel of Your kindness. Let my small acts of sharing create space for conversation, understanding, and genuine connection.

Thank You for walking with me through ordinary days and using ordinary moments to do meaningful work. I place my heart in Your hands and ask You to keep it soft, aware, and willing. May my life quietly reflect Your love, one small act at a time.

I trust You to keep guiding me, teaching me, and loving others through me.
Amen.

CHAPTER 25
Jesus Values Faith Over Perfection

SMALL MOMENTS. BIG GOD

"God isn't asking for performance--He's asking for a life that reflects His heart. To do justice, to love mercy, to walk humbly with Him… these aren't grand gestures, they're daily choices. Jesus shows up in the way you treat people, the compassion you extend, and the quiet humility that guides your steps. This is faith lived simply, honestly, and well."
SCRIPTURE: Micah 6:8

FOCUS: He isn't asking you to perform--just to walk humbly, love well, and trust Him with the rest.

Many people feel pressure to appear perfect in their spiritual lives, believing they must always have strong faith or make no mistakes. This message reminds us that Jesus does not expect perfection. Instead, He values sincere faith -- the willingness to trust Him even while we are still learning and growing.

Faith includes moments of doubt, struggle, and imperfection. Jesus understands human weakness and meets us with grace rather than judgment. What matters most is a heart that continues to seek Him, even after failure or discouragement. Each attempt to trust, forgive, or try again becomes an expression of real faith.

This reflection encourages freedom from unrealistic expectations. Spiritual growth is not about flawless performance but about honest relationship with God. When we focus on faith instead of perfection, we experience peace and confidence, knowing that Jesus works through imperfect people to accomplish meaningful transformation.

And maybe I spent too many years trying to get everything right -- trying to say the right words, make the right choices, show the right strength, as if Jesus was grading me on flawless performance instead of sincere faith. But the more I walk with Him, the more I realize He's never asked me to be perfect. He's asked me to trust Him. Perfection exhausts me. Faith restores me. Perfection isolates me. Faith draws me closer. Perfection demands I carry everything alone. Faith reminds me I was never meant to.

Jesus isn't impressed by my polished moments -- He's moved by my honest ones. The ones where I show up trembling but willing. The ones where I whisper "help me" instead of pretending I'm fine.

The ones where I take a small step forward even when fear is still tugging at my ankles. He values the faith that wobbles. The faith that questions but keeps seeking. The faith that feels small but still reaches for Him. The faith that doesn't always look strong but refuses to let go. And every time I choose faith over perfection, I feel the pressure lift. I feel grace settle. I feel His love meets me exactly where I am -- not where I think I should be. I'm learning that faith has never required me to have everything figured out. It doesn't ask me to silence my questions or pretend uncertainty doesn't exist. Doubt still shows up, sometimes unexpectedly, sometimes loudly. But faith isn't the absence of those moments--it's what I choose to do in the middle of them. It's choosing trust when clarity hasn't arrived yet.

Faith looks like leaning in instead of pulling away. It's staying open to God even when my thoughts feel scattered and my confidence feels thin. I'm discovering that God is not threatened by my questions or disappointed by my hesitation. He doesn't ask me to be flawless or fearless--He asks me to be honest. He honors the heart that keeps turning toward Him, even when it's unsure.

For a long time, I thought strong faith meant having fewer doubts. But now I see that real faith is built by bringing those doubts into God's presence instead of hiding them. Trust grows not because uncertainty disappears, but because I learn, over time, that God is steady even when I am not.

God is patient with my process. He doesn't rush me past the places where I wrestle or shame me for needing reassurance. He meets me there. And each time I choose to trust Him--quietly, imperfectly, sometimes trembling--something deeper takes root. Faith becomes less about appearances and more about relationship.

I'm learning that pretending to be strong has never impressed God. What draws Him close is a heart willing to rely on Him instead of itself. Faith is not polished or performative--it's personal. It's choosing to believe that God is good, even when circumstances are confusing, and choosing to stay present with Him instead of walking away.

And slowly, almost without noticing, trust grows. Not because doubt has vanished, but because God's faithfulness has proven itself again and again. Faith becomes steadier. Less fragile. More grounded. Built not on certainty, but on a growing confidence in who God is.

I'm learning that this kind of faith--honest, leaning, imperfect--is the kind God honors most.

So, I end this chapter with this truth anchored deep in my spirit: Jesus never asked me to perform for Him. He asked me to walk with Him. He asked me to trust Him with the parts of me that are still growing, still healing, still learning. Faith is what He honors. Faith is what He blesses. Faith is what He uses. Jesus values faith over perfection -- and that truth frees me to keep going, even when I'm still a work in progress.

TESTIMONY

The Calm Response

There was a moment when someone spoke to me in a way that felt sharp and unkind. Their words landed heavily, and almost instantly I felt the urge to respond in the same tone. I could feel my emotions rising--the defensiveness, the desire to explain myself, the temptation to match their harshness with my own. Everything in me wanted to react, to protect my pride, and to say exactly what I was feeling.

But instead of responding right away, I paused. I took a breath and chose silence over retaliation. Remaining calm did not come naturally in that moment. It required restraint and intention. I had to resist the urge to speak from emotion and instead allow space for self-control. Though it felt uncomfortable, I stayed composed and let the moment pass without returning the hurtful words.

Time went on, and later that same person came back to me. Their demeanor had changed. With sincerity and humility, they apologized for how they had spoken. Hearing those words caught me off guard. What could have grown into lingering tension or resentment was softened by that quiet moment of grace.

As I reflected on the situation, I realized that my calm response had played a part in what followed. It wasn't about winning or proving anything--it was about choosing peace. I recognized that the ability to remain calm didn't come from my own strength alone. Jesus had been present in that moment, guiding my response and helping me choose grace instead of reaction.

That experience stayed with me because it reminded me how powerful a gentle response can be. Grace doesn't always look dramatic or bold. Sometimes it looks like silence, patience, and trust. In choosing not to respond harshly, I allowed Jesus to work in the situation in a way I could not have orchestrated myself.

That moment taught me that Jesus doesn't just teach us how to speak--He teaches us how to respond. When we invite Him into our reactions, He helps us reflect His character, even in difficult interactions. In choosing grace, I witnessed how calm can disarm conflict and how kindness can open the door to reconciliation.

It was a simple moment, but it left a lasting impression. It reminded me that even in tense conversations, Jesus is present, shaping our hearts and helping us respond in ways that reflect His love.

POEM

Jesus values faith over perfection, that's clear,
Good thing too -- I'd never make it here.
I tried to look flawless, strong, and refined,
But grace made me honest and real-minded.
He's not grading life as a test I must ace,
Just asking for trust, one step of faith.

END-OF-CHAPTER QUESTIONS

1. In what areas of your life do you feel pressure to be perfect?
2. How can accepting God's grace help you release unrealistic expectations of yourself?
3. When have you experienced growth through faith even after making mistakes?
4. How does focusing on progress instead of perfection change your outlook?
5. What is one way you can practice trusting God more instead of striving to be flawless?

CLOSING PRAYER

Jesus,

Thank You for being with me in moments when my emotions rise and my patience feels thin. You know how quickly my heart wants to react when I feel hurt, misunderstood, or spoken to harshly. Thank You for gently reminding me that I don't have to respond the way the world does. Thank You for offering me another way--Your way.

Lord, I confess that staying calm is not always easy. My first instinct is often to defend myself, to answer sharp words with sharp words, and to protect my pride. Forgive me for the times I have spoken from hurt instead of love. Teach me to pause, to breathe, and to invite You into my reactions before I speak.

Jesus, thank You for helping me choose grace when it doesn't come naturally. Thank You for placing Your peace within me when everything in me wants to respond out of emotion. In moments when silence feels uncomfortable and restraint feels costly, remind me that You are working even when I am quiet.

Help me trust that You see every situation clearly. When I choose gentleness over retaliation, remind me that I am not weak--I am being shaped. When I choose calm over conflict, remind me that You are present, guiding my heart and my words. Let my responses reflect Your love, even when I feel wounded.

Lord, soften my heart so that I don't harden toward others. Teach me to respond with compassion, even when it's undeserved. Help me remember that the way I respond can either close a door or open one. Give me the wisdom to choose words--or silence--that invite peace.

Jesus, thank You for reminding me that grace has power. Thank You for showing me that calm can disarm anger, and kindness can make space for repentance and healing. I am grateful that You work through my obedience, even in moments that seem small and unnoticed.

I place my heart in Your hands. Shape my reactions. Guard my words. Teach me to reflect You in how I respond to others, especially when it's difficult. I want my life to quietly point to You--not just in what I say, but in how I choose to act.

I trust You, Jesus, to continue teaching me grace, one moment at a time.
Amen.

CHAPTER 26
Jesus Works Through Compassion

SMALL MOMENTS. BIG GOD

"Life gets heavy, and God never intended for you to shoulder everything alone. When you help lift someone else's burden--through a prayer, a listening ear, a quiet act of kindness--you're living out the heart of Jesus. And when others help carry yours, that's His love reaching back toward you. This is how grace moves through community: one shared load at a time."
SCRIPTURE: Galatians 6:2

FOCUS: When we lift each other's burdens, His love becomes visible. Compassion is one of the ways He moves through us.

Compassion is one of the simplest yet most powerful ways Jesus works through our lives. This message reminds us that caring for others -- especially during their difficult moments -- reflects God's love in practical and meaningful ways. Acts of understanding, patience, and kindness can bring comfort that words alone cannot provide.

Jesus often reaches people through human connection. When we choose empathy instead of judgment or offer help without expecting recognition, we become part of His work. Small gestures, such as listening, encouraging, or offering support, can ease someone's burden and remind them they are not alone.

This reflection encourages us to live with open hearts. Compassion does not require perfection or great resources; it simply requires willingness to care. As we respond to others with love and understanding, we discover that Jesus is actively working through those moments, turning ordinary acts of kindness into expressions of grace and healing.

And maybe I used to underestimate compassion -- thinking it was too gentle to make a difference, too quiet to shift anything, too soft to carry real power. But Jesus keeps showing me that compassion is one of His strongest tools. It reaches places correction can't. It heals wounds judgment only deepens. It opens hearts that fear has closed.

Compassion is how He moves toward people. It's how He sees them. It's how He lifts them. It's how He reminds them they're still loved, still valued, still held. And the beautiful thing is this: He doesn't just show compassion -- He works through it. Through the person who pauses long enough to listen. Through the one who chooses kindness over convenience. Through the one who offers grace instead of criticism. Through the one who shows up with gentleness when the world expects hardness.

Jesus uses compassion to soften what's been hardened, to restore what's been broken, to comfort what's been hurting, to reach what's been overlooked. And sometimes the compassion He works through isn't loud or dramatic. Sometimes it's a small gesture, a quiet word, a simple act of care that seems insignificant in the moment but becomes a lifeline to someone who needed it more than they could say. I'm learning that compassion is one of the most tangible ways God's love shows up in the world. It's how His heart becomes visible through human hands and willing hearts. Compassion doesn't always arrive with answers or solutions--it often comes simply as presence. As noticing. As choosing to see someone where they are instead of where we think they should be.

God uses compassion to enter places that feel too heavy, too broken, or too dark for words. It's there when pain feels overwhelming and hope feels distant. Sometimes it looks like listening without fixing. Sometimes it looks like staying when walking away would be easier. Compassion carries God's light into spaces where judgment would only deepen the shadows.

I've learned that compassion costs something. It asks me to slow down, to soften my heart, to allow myself to feel what I might rather avoid. But in those moments, something holy happens. God works through that willingness. He uses compassion to heal wounds I can't see and to speak comfort I don't know how to offer on my own.

Compassion doesn't erase suffering, but it reminds us that suffering is not unseen. It tells weary hearts, You matter. You are not alone here. In a world that often rushes past pain, compassion becomes a quiet declaration of God's nearness. It reflects His love in a way that feels real and reachable.

I'm learning that when I choose compassion--whether I'm offering it or receiving it--I'm standing in the flow of God's grace. He uses it to soften hard places, to restore dignity, and to bring light where despair has taken root. Compassion may seem small, but in God's hands, it becomes powerful.

And sometimes, the compassion God uses most is the kind He teaches me to extend to myself. To acknowledge my own limits. To treat my own wounds with kindness. Even there, His love becomes tangible.

May you recognize compassion as one of the ways God is near. May you feel His love through gentle presence, both given and received. And may God use compassion--yours and others'--to bring light into every dark place you encounter.

So, I end this chapter with this truth resting deeply in my spirit: Compassion is not weakness -- it's ministry. It's not optional -- it's transformative. It's not just something Jesus shows -- it's something He uses. And when I choose compassion, I'm not just being kind -- I'm partnering with Him. I'm becoming a vessel He can work through, a reminder of His heart in a world that desperately needs it.

TESTIMONY

The Neighbor Check

I began to realize that I hadn't seen my neighbor in quite some time. At first, I didn't think much of it, assuming they were simply busy or keeping to themselves. Still, the thought lingered in my mind, returning again and again as a gentle reminder I couldn't quite shake. Eventually, I decided to stop by and check on them, just to make sure everything was okay.

When I did, I discovered they had been sick and quietly struggling. They shared that they hadn't felt well enough to leave the house and were worried about getting the medicine they needed. What I thought would be a brief visit quickly became something more meaningful. I offered to pick up their medication, and the relief they expressed made it clear that this small act meant far more than I had realized.

That simple visit--just taking the time to notice and respond--turned out to be exactly what they needed in that moment. It wasn't a grand gesture or a carefully planned act of kindness. It was simply showing up, listening, and offering help where it was needed most. As I reflected on the experience, I was reminded how often Jesus works through small moments of obedience. Sometimes loving others begins with paying attention and responding to a quiet nudge in our hearts. A simple check-in, a willingness to help, or a brief visit can become a source of comfort and provision for someone else.

That experience reminded me that love doesn't always arrive loudly or dramatically. Often, it shows up through presence, compassion, and practical care. When we choose to notice the needs around us and respond with kindness, we allow Jesus to work through us--turning ordinary moments into meaningful expressions of His love.

POEM

Jesus works through compassion, simple and true,
Like helping someone when I'm tired too.
A kind word given when patience is thin,
Somehow brings peace rushing in.
Love shows up in the smallest action,
And mercy becomes heaven's attraction.

END-OF-CHAPTER QUESTIONS

1. When have you experienced compassion from someone during a difficult time?
2. How can showing empathy to others reflect your faith in everyday life?
3. What situations challenge your ability to respond with patience and understanding?
4. How can small acts of kindness make a meaningful difference in someone's day?
5. What is one intentional way you can practice compassion toward someone this week?

CLOSING PRAYER

Jesus,
Thank You for the way You quietly nudge my heart to notice others. Thank You for the moments when You slow me down just enough to see what I might otherwise miss. When I realized my neighbor had been absent, You stirred concern within me, and I'm grateful for that gentle prompting. Thank You for reminding me that love often begins with simply paying attention.

Lord, forgive me for the times I overlook the needs around me because life feels busy or distracting. Teach me to be more aware, more present, and more willing to respond when You place someone on my heart. Help me trust that when You prompt me to reach out, it is never without purpose.

Jesus, thank You for showing me that a small visit can carry great meaning. What felt like a simple check-in became a moment of provision and comfort. Thank You for allowing me to be part of what someone else needed in that moment. Remind me that I don't have to have all the answers or do something extraordinary--sometimes showing up is enough.

Soften my heart, Lord, so that I remain sensitive to Your voice. When You whisper, "Go," give me the courage to respond without hesitation. When You say, "Stay," help me be present. Let my love for others be practical, sincere, and guided by compassion rather than convenience.

Jesus, I want to be someone who notices--the quiet absences, the subtle struggles, the unspoken needs. Help me love my neighbors the way You love them, with care that is patient, thoughtful, and willing to serve. Teach me to see each interaction as an opportunity to reflect Your kindness.

Thank You for using ordinary moments to do meaningful work. Thank You for trusting me with small acts of care that can bring relief, encouragement, and hope. I place my heart in Your hands and ask You to keep it open, attentive, and responsive to those around me.

Continue to guide my steps, Lord. Use me where I am, with what I have, and in ways that bring Your love into the everyday lives of others.

I trust You, Jesus, to keep teaching me how to love--one small moment at a time.
Amen.

CHAPTER 27

Jesus Is Creating Something New Quietly

SMALL MOMENTS. BIG GOD

"You may not see movement, but that doesn't mean God is still. He specializes in new beginnings--right in the middle of dry seasons and worn-out places. Jesus is carving out paths you didn't expect and causing life to spring up where you thought nothing could grow. The new thing isn't coming… it's already starting."
SCRIPTURE: Isaiah 43:19

FOCUS: He doesn't always announce the shift--sometimes the miracle starts beneath the surface, growing in silence until it's ready to break through.

Change does not always happen in loud or noticeable ways. Often, Jesus works quietly beneath the surface, shaping new beginnings long before we can see the results. This message reminds us that even when life feels still or unchanged, God may be preparing something meaningful within us and around us.

Quiet seasons can feel confusing because progress is not always visible. Yet during these times, growth is taking place through reflection, healing, and renewed understanding. Jesus gently reshapes our thoughts, strengthens our character, and prepares us for new opportunities at the right time. What seems like silence is often a period of careful transformation.

This reflection encourages patience and trust. Instead of rushing the process, we are invited to believe that God's work continues even when it is unseen. By embracing quiet seasons, we learn that new beginnings often start softly, and Jesus faithfully creates something new in ways that unfold gradually and purposefully.

And maybe I expected new beginnings to arrive with noise -- a big announcement, a sudden shift, a moment so obvious I couldn't miss it. But Jesus rarely works that way with me. He moves like morning light, slowly stretching across the room, changing everything before I even realize the darkness has lifted. He creates new things quietly. In the thoughts that soften. In the habits that shift. In the desires that return after being numb for too long. In the courage that rises in places where fear used to live.

Sometimes the new thing He's building doesn't look like a miracle at first. It looks like peace where there used to be panic. It looks like clarity where there used to be confusion. It looks like rest where there used to be striving. It looks like a small step forward that doesn't feel dramatic but is actually evidence that something inside me is healing.

Jesus doesn't rush the process. He doesn't force growth. He doesn't pressure me to see what He's doing before I'm ready. He simply keeps working -- faithfully, patiently, quietly -- until the new thing He planted in me becomes impossible to ignore. And when I finally notice it, I realize He's been rebuilding me from the inside out, long before anything changed on the outside. I'm learning that God often begins His work in ways that are easy to miss. He doesn't always announce what He's doing with noise or urgency. Sometimes He starts with a whisper so gentle I have to slow down just to notice it. A small nudge in my heart. A subtle shift in perspective. A seed planted so quietly that I don't realize anything has changed at all.

God seems to love quiet beginnings. He works patiently, allowing growth to happen beneath the surface before anything is visible. Like a seed hidden in the soil, His work often starts in darkness--unseen, unnoticed, and seemingly still. But just because I can't see it yet doesn't mean nothing is happening. Life is forming. Roots are growing. Something new is taking shape.

There are seasons when I wish God would move faster or make His plans clearer. I want proof that progress is happening, reassurance that I'm not standing still. But God often chooses the slow sunrise over the sudden flash of light. He lets hope rise gradually, warming my heart little by little, teaching me to trust Him in the waiting.

I'm learning that God doesn't rush creation. He allows time for growth because what develops slowly tends to last. What He builds quietly is often the most enduring. Even when I feel unsure or impatient, He is steady--working with wisdom and care, shaping what's coming next in ways I couldn't orchestrate on my own.

Sometimes the most faithful thing I can do is trust that God is creating something new, even when I can't see it yet. To believe that the whisper matters. That the small beginning counts. That the slow progress is still progress.

God is present in the gentle start, the hidden work, the early light that hasn't fully broken through. And one day, I'll look back and realize that what felt like stillness was actually preparation--that the quiet was never empty, but full of His careful, creative work.

So, I end this chapter with this truth resting gently in my spirit: New beginnings don't always start with noise. Sometimes they start with a whisper. Sometimes they start with a shift so subtle only Jesus could have orchestrated it. He is creating something new in me -- quietly, carefully, consistently -- and one day, I'll look back and see that the quiet work was the most powerful work of all.

TESTIMONY

The Door Held Open

As I walked through a doorway, I noticed someone hurrying behind me. Without thinking much about it, I paused and held the door open so they could pass through. It was a small gesture, something I've done many times before, and I didn't give it much thought at first. But as they walked by, they stopped, looked at me, and thanked me sincerely.

Then they added something that caught me off guard. They said that people rarely show kindness like that anymore. Their words were simple, but they lingered with me long after the moment passed. What had felt like an ordinary act of courtesy had clearly meant more to them than I realized.

As I continued on my way, I reflected on how small actions can carry unexpected weight. Holding a door didn't cost me anything--it took only a few extra seconds--but it reminded someone that kindness still exists. In a world where people often rush past one another, even the simplest gesture can stand out.

That moment reminded me that Jesus often works through quiet, everyday acts of consideration. Small courtesies can become gentle reminders of goodness, respect, and care. When we choose to slow down and extend kindness, even in the simplest ways, we reflect His love in places we might never expect.

Sometimes it's not grand gestures that make the biggest impact, but small moments of thoughtfulness. A held door, a kind word, or a moment of patience can quietly restore hope and remind others that goodness is still present in the world. In that brief exchange, I was reminded that Jesus uses even the smallest acts of kindness to touch hearts and point people back to love.

POEM

Jesus is creating something new quietly,
While I keep asking, "Lord, is it done yet?" anxiously.
I look for fireworks, big and loud,
He works softly behind the cloud.
What feels like silence is work in view,
Because quiet seasons grow something new.

END-OF-CHAPTER QUESTIONS

1. What areas of your life feel quiet or uncertain right now, yet may be part of new growth?
2. How can trusting God help you remain patient when change is not immediately visible?
3. What lessons have you learned during seasons that felt slow or silent?
4. How might God be preparing you internally for something new ahead?
5. What is one way you can remain hopeful while waiting for new beginnings to unfold?

CLOSING PRAYER

Jesus,
Thank You for the small moments You use to remind me that kindness still has power. Thank You for the quiet opportunities You place in my path--moments so ordinary they could easily be overlooked. Holding a door, pausing for someone else, offering a small courtesy--You show me that even these simple acts can carry meaning far beyond what I see.

Lord, forgive me for the times I rush through life without noticing the people around me. So often I am focused on where I'm going next that I miss the chance to slow down and extend kindness. Teach me to be more aware, more present, and more willing to pause when love calls me to do so.

Jesus, thank You for reminding me that goodness still matters in a weary world. When someone said that kindness feels rare, it stirred something in my heart. Help me remember that even the smallest act of courtesy can restore hope and remind someone they are seen. Use my words, my actions, and my presence to reflect Your goodness in places where it may feel absent.

Help me, Lord, to choose kindness even when it costs me a few extra seconds. Let my heart remain soft in a world that often feels hurried and hardened. Teach me to respond with patience, gentleness, and compassion, especially when no one is watching and nothing is expected in return.

Jesus, I want my life to quietly point to You--not through grand gestures, but through consistent love in small ways. Let my actions speak of Your grace. Let my presence bring peace. Let my everyday choices remind others that goodness is still alive and love still exists.

Thank You for walking with me through ordinary moments and turning them into opportunities for grace. Keep my heart attentive to Your voice and my hands ready to serve. I place my life in Your care and ask You to continue shaping me through small acts of love. I trust You, Jesus, to use even the simplest kindness for Your greater purpose.
Amen.

CHAPTER 28
Jesus Has Been Present All Along

SMALL MOMENTS. BIG GOD

"Before you step into a new season, Jesus is already there. Before you face the hard thing, He's standing in the middle of it. He goes ahead of you, stays beside you, and guards what's behind you. Even when courage feels thin, His presence is thick around your life. You don't have to fear the unknown when the One who knows everything walks with you."
SCRIPTURE: Deuteronomy 31:8

FOCUS: Even when the path felt uncertain, He was already ahead of you--steady, faithful, and guiding every step.

There are moments in life when we feel alone, confused, or unsure of where God is leading us. Looking back, however, we often realize that Jesus was present even during the times we could not recognize Him. This message reminds us that God's guidance is constant, even when circumstances make His presence difficult to see.

Throughout challenges, transitions, and unexpected changes, Jesus quietly walks beside us, offering strength, protection, and direction. What once seemed like random events or unanswered questions may later reveal purpose and growth. His presence is not always obvious in the moment, but it becomes clearer through reflection and understanding over time.

This reflection encourages trust in God's faithfulness. Even when we doubt or struggle, Jesus remains near, working through every experience to shape our journey. Realizing that He has been present all along brings comfort and gratitude, helping us move forward with confidence, knowing we have never truly walked alone.

And maybe I didn't always see Him. Not because He wasn't there, but because life was loud, my heart was tired, and my eyes were focused on surviving the moment in front of me. But when I look back now -- with a little more clarity, a little more healing, a little more honesty -- I can trace His presence through every season I thought I walked alone.

He was there in the moments I didn't have the words to pray. He was there in the nights I cried quietly so no one would hear. He was there in the decisions I made with trembling hands. He was there in the doors that closed, the ones that opened, and the ones I didn't understand until much later.

Jesus has never been distant. He has never been indifferent. He has never been late. He has been steady -- guiding, protecting, comforting, correcting, and carrying me in ways I didn't recognize at the time. Sometimes His presence looked like strength I didn't know I had. Sometimes it looked like peace that made no sense. Sometimes it looked like a person who showed up at the exact moment I needed support. Sometimes it looked like a closed path that saved me from something I didn't see coming.

And even in the seasons where I felt forgotten, He was working behind the scenes, holding things together, holding me together, until I was strong enough to see His fingerprints on the story. There were moments in my life when I didn't recognize God's presence at all. Seasons when I felt alone, unsure, or convinced that I was navigating everything on my own. Looking back now, I see how incomplete my perspective was. God was there--even when I didn't know how to look for Him, even when I didn't feel Him near. He was present in ways I couldn't yet understand, steady in moments I thought were empty.

God's faithfulness doesn't depend on my awareness of it. He remains when I'm distracted, weary, or questioning. He stays close through confusion, through growth, through the quiet unfolding of days that don't feel significant at the time. Long before I could name His work, He was already doing it--guiding, protecting, sustaining me with a patience I didn't yet appreciate.

I'm learning that God's presence is not fragile. It doesn't come and go based on my faithfulness or clarity. He is constant when I am inconsistent. Near when I feel distant. Faithful when I struggle to believe He is. His nearness has been woven through every chapter of my story, even the ones I misunderstood or wished away.

Now, when I look back, I can see the traces of His care everywhere--in the strength that appeared when I had none left, in the doors that quietly closed for my good, in the unseen protection that only became clear with time. What once felt like absence was often preparation. What felt like silence was still love at work.

God is not only the One who was there--He is the One who remains. Present today. Faithful still. Always closer than I realize. And as I continue forward, I'm learning to trust that the same God who never left me then will not leave me now.

So, I end this chapter with this truth anchored deep in my spirit: Jesus was there when I didn't notice Him. He was there when I doubted Him. He was there when I questioned everything. He was there when I felt lost, weary, or unseen.

He has been present all along -- quietly faithful, endlessly patient, and deeply invested in every detail of my life. And now that I can see it, I walk forward with a different kind of confidence -- not in myself, but in the God who never left.

TESTIMONY

The Simple Thank You

I took a moment to thank someone for a small thing they had done for me. It wasn't anything major--just a simple act that made my day a little easier. I didn't think much of it when I spoke the words, but their response caught me by surprise. They paused, looked at me, and quietly said that no one had shown them appreciation in a long time.

That brief comment stayed with me. What I had offered so casually--a sincere thank-you--had touched something deeper in them than I realized. It made me aware of how often people go unnoticed, even when they are consistently helping, serving, or showing up for others. Sometimes people aren't looking for recognition, but they still long to know that what they do matters.

As I reflected on that moment, I realized how powerful gratitude can be. A few kind words, spoken honestly, have the ability to lift a weary spirit and remind someone they are seen. In that exchange, we were both encouraged--the one who received appreciation and the one who gave it.

That small interaction reminded me that gratitude is more than good manners; it is a gift. When we take the time to acknowledge others, we allow Jesus to work through our words in quiet but meaningful ways. Appreciation can heal places we didn't even know were hurting and strengthen connections we didn't realize were fragile.

In that moment, I was reminded that gratitude doesn't have to be grand to be impactful. A simple "thank you" can become a blessing, offering encouragement where it's been missing. Jesus often uses these small expressions of kindness to spread His love--touching both hearts involved and reminding us that even our simplest words can carry grace.

POEM

Jesus has been present all along, I see,
Even in moments that confused me.
I thought I was walking life alone,
Then realized His footprints matched my own.
Through every twist where I felt wrong,
He was guiding me quietly all along.

END-OF-CHAPTER QUESTIONS

1. Looking back, when have you realized God was guiding you even when you did not recognize it at the time?
2. How have past challenges helped shape your faith or personal growth?
3. What moments in your life now seem clearer when viewed with hindsight?
4. How can remembering God's past faithfulness strengthen your trust today?
5. What is one way you can become more aware of God's presence in your current season?

CLOSING PRAYER

Jesus,
Thank You for reminding me of the power carried in simple words. Thank You for moments when You slow me down and prompt me to notice the people around me--the ones who quietly give, serve, and help without expecting recognition. I'm grateful that You gently remind me how much a sincere "thank you" can mean.

Lord, I confess that there are times I benefit from the kindness of others without fully acknowledging it. Forgive me for moments when I move on too quickly, forgetting that encouragement and appreciation can breathe life into a weary heart. Teach me to be more intentional with my gratitude and more aware of the impact my words can have.

Jesus, thank You for showing me that appreciation is a gift that blesses both the giver and the receiver. In that simple exchange, You reminded me that people often carry unseen weariness--longing to be noticed, valued, and affirmed. Help me remember that my words have the power to lift someone who feels overlooked or forgotten.

Shape my heart, Lord, so that gratitude flows naturally from me. Let me be quick to acknowledge goodness, faithfulness, and kindness in others. Help me speak words that encourage rather than remain silent. Teach me to reflect Your love through sincere appreciation, even when the act being thanked feels small or ordinary.

Jesus, I want my gratitude to be rooted in humility. Remind me that everything I receive--every kindness, every helping hand--is a reflection of Your grace working through others. Let my thankfulness always point back to You and draw my heart closer to

Yours. Help me slow down enough to see people clearly. Let my words be intentional and my gratitude genuine. Use my simple expressions of appreciation to bring encouragement, healing, and reassurance to hearts that may be tired or discouraged. Thank You for being a God who notices every act of love, no matter how small. Thank You for teaching me that gratitude can become a form of ministry--one that costs little but gives much. I place my heart in Your hands and ask You to continue shaping me into someone who reflects Your kindness through both actions and words.

I trust You, Jesus, to keep reminding me of the beauty found in gratitude and the quiet strength it brings. Amen.

ABOUT THE AUTHOR

Geraldine E. Watson-Marriott is a woman of strong faith, deep gratitude, and a joyful Caribbean spirit. Raised with values rooted in prayer, perseverance, and community, she believes that life itself is a testimony of God's grace. Her writing reflects the warmth, resilience, and hope often found in Jamaican culture -- where faith, laughter, and strength help people move through both good times and difficult seasons.

Geraldine has always believed that God speaks not only through powerful sermons or big life-changing moments, but also through everyday experiences. From quiet prayers in the early morning to conversations with family and friends, she has learned that some of God's greatest lessons come through ordinary situations. These small moments have shaped her faith and inspired her desire to write words that encourage, comfort, and uplift others.

Known for her caring heart and uplifting spirit, Geraldine enjoys sharing stories that remind people to keep trusting God, even when the path is unclear. She understands that life brings challenges, but she also believes joy can still be found through faith, gratitude, and a sense of humor. Her island background influences her voice -- warm, welcoming, and filled with encouragement that feels like sitting with someone who truly understands life's journey.

Writing became a way for her to share hope and to remind others that they are never alone. Through her work, she seeks to reach readers who may feel overlooked, tired, or uncertain, helping them recognize that God is present in every detail of their lives. Her message is simple: nothing is too small for God's attention, and every moment carries purpose.

In Jesus in the Small Stuff, Geraldine invites readers to slow down and notice the blessings hidden in daily living. Her prayer is that each person who reads this book will feel encouraged, strengthened, and reminded that faith is not only about mountaintop experiences, but about trusting God step by step, day by day.